The Devil's Picturebook

The Devil's Picturebook

The Compleat Guide to Tarot Cards: Their Origins and Their Usage

With illustrations by the author

Paul Huson

G.P. Putnam's Sons   New York

By the author of
MASTERING WITCHCRAFT

Copyright©1971 by Paul Huson

Library of Congress Catalog Card Number: 72-157064

PRINTED IN THE UNITED STATES OF AMERICA

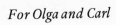

For Olga and Carl

I spread before me now the forty cards,
Yet 'tis not forty cards which here I spread,
But forty of the gods superior
To the deity Laverna, that their forms
May each and all become volcanoes hot
Until Laverna comes and brings my child;
And 'til 'tis done may they all cast at her
Hot flames of fire, and with them glowing coals
From noses, mouths and ears (until she yields);
Then may they leave Laverna to her peace,
Free to embrace her children at her will!

—C. G. Leland, *Aradia, or the Gospel of the Witches*

Contents

Foreword

Whether you know it or not, each time you pick up a deck of playing cards you are putting your soul in immediate danger of hellfire. So the church once said. The tarot was the medieval prototype for our present-day deck. Instead of hearts, diamonds, spades and clubs, it used cups, coins, swords and batons as symbols. In addition, it also contained a series of twenty-two mysterious picture cards called trumps. The main use for tarot cards, apart from simple gambling, was for telling fortunes. This was their true danger. Worse still, within the cards lurked devils disguised as kings and heroes. To quote a seventeenth-century moralist on this point:

> The playe of Cards is an invention of the Devill, which he found out, that he might the easier bring in ydolatrie amongst men. *For the King and Coate* [Court] *cards that we use now were in olde times the images of idols and false gods:* which since, they that would seeme Christians, have changed into Charlemaigne, Launcelot, Hector and such like names, because they would not seeme to imitate their idolatrie therein, and yet maintain the playe itself.

This indicates the connection between playing cards and witchcraft. That witches practiced rites drawn from old pagan cults is becoming more and more a matter of common knowledge. That remnants of these old cults have boldly remained on display for all to see down the ages is not so well known.

Anthropologists generally recognize two fruitful places to search for such pagan remnants. First, within the contemporary religions, in this case Christianity. Here the gods and spirits of the old cults often will be found to have become rewoven into the fabric of the new, often as saints, like Saint Bride and Saint Nicholas, ministering angels, like Saint Michael, and demons, like the devil himself.

Second, they can be looked for in the field of folklore and apparently meaningless traditional games still played in outlying country districts. Many of these games now lack meaning, because they are the descendants of old religious customs; often the game may have dramatized some occurrence in a deity's life. It may have involved feats of strength on the part of the players or merely required that dice be cast or entrails be inspected. But the aim was always similar: to involve the players in the "life" and immediate intentions of the deity, whether seen as a god or simply as mysterious fate. Whether it was a Babylonian haruspicy, a gladiatorial match, a chivalric joust or a trial by ordeal, gods were always involved, manipulating the laws of chance, although, of course, they were only apparent to those who had eyes to see them. Any gambler can still tell you that today: the human players merely cast the dice; Lady Luck and her associates arrange the outcome.

Such thinking was the real danger to the churches, for it suggested that there were other powers than the Christian God in control. The word "sorcery" actually derives from the Latin *sortilegium*, meaning to cast lots. The old Semitic word for sorcery, *naib*, simply refers to card play.

The chief aim of this book is twofold: first, to teach the reader how to tell fortunes with tarot cards; and second, to explain where the cards originated and what they came to mean to those who used them most, the sorcerer and sorceress. Maybe we shall find that the old Puritan epithet "Devil's Picturebook" was not such a slur after all.

Talking Tarot – A Glossary of Terms

Before even beginning, let me give you a list of some of the technical tarot terms that you will encounter in the following chapters. Most of them are explained as a matter of course. However, in order not to have to keep referring back, this glossary should supply a quick guide to them in time of need.

Arcana—Major and Minor: the two broad divisions of the tarot pack. The Major Arcana consists of twenty-two allegorical trumps; the Minor of fifty-six suit cards.

Cabala—(1) Body of Judaic lore stemming from early Chaldean and Mesopotamian traditions, later incorporated in certain rabbinical texts such as the *Zohar*. (2) Practical occult processes deriving from these.

Cartomancy—Prophecy or fortune-telling by means of cards, tarot or the regular playing cards.

Divination—Any type of fortune-telling or prophecy which makes use of a ritual, such as cartomancy.

Glyph—Occult symbol.

Layout—Same as spread. Pattern of cards dealt out in cartomancy.

Nota—Occult symbol associated with the spirit or demon. His "signature" or sigil.

Numerology—Occult science of numbers whereby each number

is assigned a special symbolic meaning and mystical power.

Querent—Person who is consulting the cards.

Rosicrucian—Belonging to a body of occult lore originally derived from pagan sources but rewoven into a Christian doctrine during the Renaissance.

Significator—Card chosen in a fortune-telling spread to symbolize the querent himself.

Spread—See Layout.

Tarot—Fortune-telling pack of seventy-eight cards.

Trump—Generally a card of the Major Arcana (*q.v.*). There are, however, several types of trumps:

Five Greater Trumps:	The Star
	The Moon
	The Sun
	The Judgment
	The World
Five Lesser Trumps	The Juggler
	The Female Pope
	The Empress
	The Emperor
	The Pope
Seven Tarot Trumps:	The Fool
	The Juggler
	The World
	The King of Rods
	The King of Swords
	The King of Cups
	The King of Coins

(The four kings are only referred to as "trumps" when employed in the game of trumps or triumphs.)

CHAPTER 1

Reading the Cards

The first question anyone will ask you if you ever let it be known that you are interested in tarot cards is, "Can you tell my fortune?" If you admit that you actually own a deck, then of course the request becomes a demand. For what is the use of owning a deck of tarots if you don't know how to use it?

Therefore, before embarking on a study of the deeper and darker aspects of tarot cards, you will quite obviously need to know how to use them in the way that the average tarot enthusiast does: as fortune-telling devices.

The origin of fortune-telling by cards dates back many centuries. In the past it was taken very seriously by the illiterate diviner, for it was a method of finding out one's future by means of pictures and thus eliminated the need for being able to read and write. The more educated practitioner generally relied on more sophisticated methods of divination, such as astrology. He used the tarot as well, but in a slightly different way.

But how can rational persons in our day believe that a deck of playing cards could in any way accurately reveal the future or the solution to a knotty problem? If they do, and many highly intelligent people believe they do, then the key to the riddle of why the tarots should work probably lies within the mind of man himself rather than in the cards. Basically, the tarot cards are nothing more than mirrors in which, if you know consciously aware of, but which the deeper, unconscious part of your mind in some mysterious manner already knows.

We shall look into the "whys" of this process later; for the moment let us consider the "how."

Getting to know your cards

Before you can begin reading tarot cards, you obviously must first obtain a deck if you don't already have one. Not only must the deck appeal to you, but the card designs must be striking enough to impress themselves upon your imagination sufficiently to transform them into effective deep mind mirrors. So when you begin looking for a tarot deck, give yourself a chance to select one of which you approve. Don't buy the first one you happen upon. You must end up buying one which satisfies you and only you. Ideally, one should design and make a deck oneself. With this in mind, many devoted tarot practitioners obtain the Paul Foster Case deck in black and white line drawing and paint them in themselves, like a child's coloring book. The principle behind this is one of identification. Your tarot deck must become part of you. However, if you don't feel up to making or inking in one for yourself, simply purchase one of the many decks available at bookstores.

In selecting one, let yourself be guided by your own instinct. If you have an eye for color, the Rosicrucian Waite-Coleman Smith deck may catch your attention. Ancient Egyptian enthusiasts will relish the pack put out by Zain, while cabalists will perhaps be more drawn to the Wirth or Harris-Crowley deck. Traditionalists will probably want to stick with the Marseilles deck or one of the Italian packs. However, whichever you decide upon, make sure the choice is *your own* and not that of the shop salesman or merely "the only pack they had left." This is most important. If you really have no preference, then choose the one which seems to catch your eye most.

Once you have bought your deck—without bargaining over the price, if you want to be true to the oldest tradition of witchcraft—take it home, set it out in front of you and take a good look at it. You will notice that it is considerably thicker than the regular deck of cards. This is because it has twenty-five more cards in it. You will see that the individual cards are also larger in size. If you have bought an English, American or French deck, you will see that the picture cards (trumps and court cards) are full-length, rather than double-headed and reversible like regular playing cards. On the other hand, if you have bought an Italian deck, you may find that the double-headed reversible card has been introduced. In this case you will have to make a small mark on the card to show which end is its top and which its bottom. When you start divining with the cards, you will find this has a relevance, for the card may have a different interpretation when upside down.

As you examine your pack, you will notice that the cards fall into five distinct sets: first there are "Coins" or "Pentacles," disklike symbols sometimes containing five-pointed stars; then there are "Swords"; "Cups" or "Chalices," gobletlike symbols; and "Rods" or "Scepters," sometimes called "Wands." The court cards also carry these mysterious symbols. They are the king or master, the queen or lady, the valet or page (the knave or jack in a regular deck) and the knight. The knight is always a man seated on horseback. In early decks he was sometimes represented as half man, half beast, like the legendary centaur. But nowadays he is shown simply as an obvious knight (Figures 1-5). The court cards are directly descended from the idea of a feudal court ruled by its lord and lady who are attended by both the favorite page, who is master of arms, and their jousting champion. In this context the lesser cards of each suit are immediately comparable to the subjects of the lord and lady, in much the same way that the pawns of a chessboard "belong" to the king and queen of their own color. Indeed, the similarities between the figures of chess and European playing cards are so striking that there have been various attempts to correlate the two systems—none has been particularly successful, however.

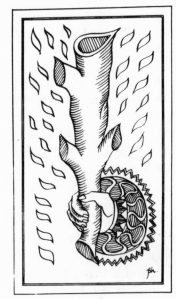

Figure 1   Figure 2

If you buy an Italian deck, you may have difficulty in distinguishing the Rods from the Swords at first. They are very similar. Just remember that the Swords generally curve in these decks, while the Rods are depicted as straight.

After checking off the four minor suits, you will see that twenty-two cards remain. These are the all-important tarot "trumps," the so-called Major Arcana. Notice that they progress from number one to twenty-one, with a single card left over— the Fool, usually left unnumbered or simply labeled zero. Often the numerals on the trumps will be Roman—the Arabic zero of the Fool being the one exception.

Having satisfied yourself as to the contents of your tarot deck and that there are indeed seventy-eight cards in it, you must now familiarize yourself with the individual cards.

One of the easiest ways to do this is simply to play games with them, either regular card games or games of make-believe.

Figure 3

Figure 4

The latter is the method by which the occult practitioner gets to know and "activates" his deck, but if you don't feel yourself able to take such a radical step back into the world of childhood yet, the former is just as effective. Exploring the tarot is always more rewarding if you can get one or two of your friends interested in participating. To play tarot games this is more or less essential, although with a little ingenuity tarot games of solitaire can be devised using the trumps as a fifth suit.

The best way to get acquainted with your cards is by playing either the game of "triumphs" ("trumps") or the simpler game of Pelmanism, the rules for which will be found at the end of this chapter.

Once you find you can distinguish the cards from one another, you may take your familiarization process a step farther. Begin associating the figures portrayed in your trump and court cards with people you know. In the case of the trumps, base

Figure 5

your classification of type upon the primary import of each card which you will find described later. For instance, you may associate the card Justice with a judge you know personally or may have faced; a lawyer or agent with the Juggler; a personal enemy of yours with the Devil; a wise counselor whose judgment you trust with the Pope. With Death you might associate a mortician; with the Empress a mother image; and with the figure standing in the Chariot someone serving in the police force or the armed services, and so on. The court cards should also be associated in this manner, but we shall list some of the types of person traditionally linked with each of them farther on.

To get the most out of your tarot deck, each one of the cards should mean something special to you. This should not begin and end with the traditional meaning ascribed to the card, but rather each should be an expression of some part of your own experience and have some special relevance for you. This is why one tarot diviner very often will not attempt to interpret the cards selected and laid out by another for a third party.

So, ideally, as a budding tarot reader who plans to take his art seriously, you should begin living with the cards, weaving their characters and the attitudes they portray into your everyday life in much the same way that a child will do with his storybook characters. One of the best ways to do this is to compose stories or playlets around each tarot trump before falling asleep at night. After closing your eyes, using the little figure or picture on the card chosen for the evening as a starting point, deliberately let your imagination wander, as you would do normally before sinking into sleep but maintaining enough alertness to guide it gently back to the central image again if once it gets too far off course. Persist in this, and you will find yourself beginning to become involved in a curious dialogue between the random images being sent up by your deep mind and the fixed point provided by the tarot picture. After a very short time you will find that the card is calling up certain associative images which will be your own personal reactions to it. Repeat this exercise on at least three successive occasions for each card, noting the recurring symbols that the image calls up. They will always be traceable to past associations and memories, but by linking them naturally with a tarot trump, you will in effect be building up your own shorthand system for divining in the manner that natural-born psychics do. Never mind that the images and ideas that drift together seem totally fabricated and arbitrary. Tarot images are archetypes and perform in a characteristic, seemingly autonomous manner when left to their own devices, apparently picking the right associations out of the storehouse of the deep mind. Deep calleth unto deep; like associates with like. This is the manner in which archetypes work. It is these associated images which will become the meanings you attach to the tarot trumps when they turn up in a reading.

When embarking on your little nocturnal fantasy trips, try to make use of *all* your imaginative senses to build your picture. Actually strive to feel the heat radiating from the solar orb depicted on the Sun, or the cold mist rising from the dew pond in the foreground of the Moon. Hear the crack of thunder and lightning playing about the turret of the Dark Tower. Really invest your imagination in the fantasy. This is where the secret of magical success lies, as any practicing witch or warlock will tell you. You may use the descriptions of the cards to be found later as guidelines to start your tarot story. Don't worry about remembering the details of the fantasy—if you happen to drift off to sleep in the middle of it, so much the better.

As you will have realized, there is no absolutely fixed meaning to any one card. Each reader will form his own interpretation based upon intuition to begin with, and later experience will enlarge upon it. This initial dream exploration process is nothing more than an incursion into the intuitive levels of your mind. You will in effect be metaphorically exploring some of the seven-eighths of the iceberg lying beneath the waterline of your consciousness. The tarot image is the one-eighth that remains above. When you begin to deal the cards for a reading, if the preliminary work of exploration and activation has been accomplished properly, the images will stir your deep mind, which in turn will start feeding up hints to you about the subject in question.

An occultist's view of the nature of reality presupposes the notion of planes or "layers" of significance and possible awareness. The higher or farther you get from the everyday here-and-now layer, the less meaning concepts such as "time and space" or "you and me" begin to have. Thus, at a certain point of ascent it is possible, according to this theory, to gain access to areas which in the here-and-now world are categorized as "someone else's memories" or "tomorrow's events," in the same way as you would your own or those recollections of yesterday. The famous speculation of John Donne that "no man is an island unto himself" from a psychic point of view is very true.

In addition to this psychic exploration of the cards, you as a beginner should also carry the cards with you as often as possible, either collectively or singly. The intent here is one of incorporating your "magnetism" in them. Far from being kept hidden and sacred, as in priestly traditions of cabalistic magic, the tarots should become an extension of you, as much a part of you as the fingers of your hand. Another very good suggestion is to sleep with them by the bed, with the card you are presently working with tucked under your pillow.

You may find the pip cards of the Minor Arcana the most difficult to deal with initially. Whereas the symbols used in the trumps and to a lesser extent the court cards are fairly obvious, those cards from two to ten in the Minor Arcana really give no hint of their meaning, except perhaps to someone familiar with numerology or the cabala.

Though not so easy to characterize, each pip card does acquire a definite personality for the tarot reader over the years. Apropos of this I should point out that the pictorial designs for pip cards shown on the tarot deck designed in the 1900's by Pamela Coleman Smith are entirely the fabrication of her colleague, Arthur Edward Waite, owing little or nothing to tarot tradition. Historically, tarot suit cards just portray an array of emblems and nothing more. However, Waite's cards will work well enough so long as the tarot reader is prepared to subscribe to the Rosicrucian doctrines from which Waite drew his inspiration. The trumps in his deck remain unmolested for the most part, and that is the important point. For the Major Arcana trumps illustrate psychic evolution and deeper states of mind.

Because of this ambiguity in interpretation, the traditional meanings are sometimes written on the face of the revelant pip cards by the beginner to aid him in remembering which meaning he has selected. But whatever meaning you settle on will be entirely up to you. There are several equally acceptable traditional interpretations to choose from. The one I shall now deal with may be the oldest. It is prevalent throughout Italy and some parts of France.

What do the cards all mean?

These are the primary meanings attached to each tarot card for the purposes of fortune-telling. Along with each definition there is an alternative interpretation to be used when the card turns up reversed in the layout. You will notice that it is frequently the opposite of its right-side-up meaning. Although this method of reading the cards is generally employed nowadays, it is a relatively modern innovation.

The Fortune-telling interpretations
attached to the trumps or Major Arcana

The Fool—anarchy, freedom, existentialism, intoxication
  Reversed—madness, carelessness, stupidity, nihilism
The Juggler, Magus or Magician—cleverness, skill, subtlety
  Reversed—deceit, thievery, lies
The Female Pope or High Priestess—The Jungian *anima*, the muse, the goddess, silence, intuition, virginity, the querent if female, the object of his affections if male
  Reversed—treachery, feminine hostility, enforced virginity, bitterness, the evil eye, the sorceress
The Empress—fertility, mother, benefactress, kindliness, health
  Reversed—dissipation, overindulgence
The Emperor—benificence,   father, benefactor, development, action
  Reversed—paternalism, tyranny, authority
The Pope, Hierophant or High Priest—the Jungian *animus*, the guardian angel or higher self, the god, spiritual counsel, wisdom, occult power, the querent if male, the object of her affections if female
  Reversed—bad advice, male hostility, the false prophet, overindulgence
The Lovers—beauty, love, attraction, emotional trial resulting in success for the querent
  Reversed—frustration in love, failure of the querent to succeed in trial
The Chariot—war, courage, victory, vengeance
  Reversed—defeat, arguments

Fortitude—self-discipline, success, action, strength
    Reversed—tyranny, obstinacy
The Hermit or the Old Man—prudence, circumspection, delay, consideration, caution
    Reversed—concealment, dissemblance, unnecessary caution, inertia
Wheel of Fortune—destiny, worldly luck, success
    Reversed—ill fortune, failure
Justice—equality, equity, balance, control
    Reversed—bigotry, bias, severity, legal complication
The Hanged Man—self-sacrifice, wisdom, intuition, divination, involvement, initiation
    Reversed—release, futile gesture of sacrifice, selfishness
Death—end, mortality, transformation
    Reversed—death, inertia, change, putrifaction
Temperance—combination, moderation, management, economy
    Reversed—discord, disunion
The Devil—unavoidable event—will turn out well
    Reversed—unavoidable event—will turn out badly
The Tower—catastrophic overthrow, usually in favor of the querent
    Reversed—catastrophe to detriment of the querent; imprisonment
The Star—hope, expectations, gifts, promises
    Reversed—false hope, false promises
The Moon—fluctuation, illusion, occult forces, intuition
    Reversed—delusions, mistakes, inconstancy, vacillation
The Sun—joy, rebirth, success
    Reversed—the same to a lesser degree
The Last Judgment or Angel—renewal, outcome, final change, result
    Reversed—delay, postponement, unsatisfactory result, sentence
The World or Universe—ultimate success, public recognition, glory, honor, reward
    Reversed—permanence, establishment

The traditional meanings of the individual cards of the Minor Arcana*

Rods

(Things to do with work and creativity)

Ace—activity, beginning, wisdom, initiative, male libido
2—novelty, turmoil, restlessness
3—cooperation, collective enterprise, good start
4—standstill, family bond, demands of society, refuge
5—wealth and success
6—domesticity
7—skillful exchange of ideas, good communication
8—stability, understanding, a rural matter
9—delays
10—treachery, undermining influence, travel
Page—bright youngster, informant, good news
Knight—change of residence, departure, emigration
Queen—astute woman, honesty, business transaction
King—clever man, honesty, good advice

Cups

(Things to do with love, pleasure, sensitivity and fertility)

Ace—passion, inspiration, pleasure, fertility, regeneration
2—loving union
3—fulfillment
4—satiety, surplus of enjoyment leading to boredom
5—inheritance, gift, something passed on
6—end of relationship, past memory, nostalgia
7—speculative fantasy
8—gentle attachment, casual association
9—total fulfillment, complete success
10—home life or homeland; cards adjacent indicate final outcome

---

*A reversed pip card generally reverses its upright meaning. If it is ominous to begin with (viz., 3 of Swords), reversal undoes its harm and may signify an end to the condition. However, a reversed court card is always hostile to the querent.

Page—sensitive youngster
Knight—lover, rival, seducer, a proposition or message
Queen—sensitive or creative woman, wife, mother
King—sensitive or creative man, benefactor, husband, father

Swords

(Things to do with stress or authority)

Ace—authority and stress
2—temporary amnesty
3—rupture, delay
4—solitude, retreat often caused by health or finance
5—loss, affliction, bereavement, defeat
6—struggle, turmoil, travel
7—hope
8—criticism
9—unmarried or unattached person, unseen complications or adversaries
10—failure, affliction
Page—a spy or rival, deceit
Knight—a fighter, struggle, strife
Queen—woman in authority, a widow, dour, sad
King—man in authority, judge or critic, severe

Coins

(Things to do with finance, economics, stability or burden)
Ace—prosperity, abundance
2—monetary obstacles, need for financial dexterity
3—status, earned esteem, honor
4—material benefits, acquisitiveness
5—"head ruled by heart," business loss through emotions
6—largesse, handout, gift, allowance
7—ardent pursuit of wealth, greed
8—prudence, economy
9—economic rewards, prudent success
10—stable home, family life, the house

Page—crass young materialist, dull person, avarice
Knight—useful person, hard worker, perseverance
Queen—wealthy woman, mother, security
King—wealthy man, father, slow deliberation, stability

Beginning to read the cards

Once you feel you have familiarized yourself with your deck of tarots, do a trial reading. You'll need a guinea pig. Ask a friend to volunteer. Find out beforehand if he has a troublesome problem, but make sure he doesn't tell you what it is. Tell him to think about it while he is drawing the cards which form the basis for his reading. Don't worry about making a fool of yourself when you start the reading. You are bound to make as many errors as hits at first, but you will soon start to get the right feeling when the cards begin "speaking" to you and triggering your intuitions correctly. This can be a very exciting moment. Your concentration will become very intense and your perception acute.

In the final analysis, it is not so much the pattern of the layout which counts but the frame of mind of the reader. Therefore, it is desirable for the reader to achieve a feeling of detached, introspective calm, a "wise passivity," as it has been called. To do this he will have to dampen down the activity of his conscious mind. The cards as they are turned up must be allowed to flow into a story. The reader will find that this will be the point at which his previously experienced fantasy associations will begin to crop up again. However, he will also find that the juxtaposition of several cards, as opposed to their single separate use, will begin to produce new aspects and new associations hitherto unexplored. Likewise, another's presence during the reading will also tend to bend the narrative in a certain direction.

In order to make a quick entry into this light state of dissociation, many tarot readers practice an initial small series of deep, rhythmic breathing exercises. If properly done, these will help your body to relax and the rhythm itself will relax the mind. Take a deep, slow breath, mentally counting to four as you do—deep enough to expand your chest, but not so deep as to cause discomfort. Hold it for another count of four, and then expel it slowly to a further steady count of four. As you reach the end of the exhalation, gently but deliberately push your stomach *out*. This forced abdominal expansion ensures the gradual relaxation of the area of your nervous system known as the solar plexus. Hold this state for yet another count of four and repeat the exercise. This rhythmic breathing can be kept up for a minute or two; the sign of success is that feeling of withdrawal similar to the one experienced before falling asleep: a sort of alert state of relaxation.

You may also find that a warm drink of tea or coffee helps greatly. Many cartomancers tend to find that most alcohol dampens the intuitive processes. Brandy, however, seems to be an exception, though its stimulus is short lived. However, again this is a matter of personal experience. Not everyone reacts the same way.

The introductory ritual

Now most, if not all, tarot readers accompany this process of "centering down" with an introductory ritual of some sort, ranging from simply choosing a "significator" or even just cutting the cards to a lengthy cabalistic invocation like "the Opening of the Key," borrowed from the Order of the Golden Dawn, whose teachings and origins we shall touch on later:

> Thee I invoke, IAO, that thou will send HRU, the Great Angel that is set over the operations of this Secret Wisdom, to lay his hand invisibly upon these consecrated cards of art, that thereby we may obtain true knowledge of hidden things, to the glory of thine ineffable Name. Amen.

This is an obviously Rosicrucian formula drawing on Gnostic sources such as the Great Name of Power, IAO. Here it is used to call upon the services of the angel HRU, probably "Heru," an old variant of the name of the Egyptian falcon-headed god Horus. In this instance, HRU represents the higher levels of being of the person consulting the cards, or the "querent." In Jungian terms one might refer to this as the "self," the inmost, transcendent portion of a person's being. However, complex prayers are not essential. Whatever your inclination, whether a committed occultist or merely someone interested in reading tarot cards, your next step is simply to choose the significator. The significator is the card which is initially decided upon by the reader to represent the inner mind of the person who is consulting the cards. When specific details such as financial events are required, thus placing the divination more in the area of mundane fortune-telling than anything else, the significator is taken from among the court cards of the Minor Arcana, which represent the outer personality rather than the inner self. This is where your early practice of mentally linking the court cards with "types" comes in handy. Some readers allow the querent to select for himself which court card will represent him. I have always felt that the choice should be in the hands of the reader, as it is in him that the chief responsibility for penetrating the unseen lies.

On the other hand, when the matter inquired about requires an in-depth, all-embracing study, then the significator should be a card representing the deep self of the inquirer. This card will be drawn from the Major Arcana, thus leaving twenty-one major cards remaining at liberty.

For a man the traditional card to choose as significator is the Pope (sometimes called the Hierophant or High Priest in modern decks); for a woman, the Female Pope (High Priestess). As we shall see later, the Pope is an old Christianized version of the sky god Jupiter, the All Father. *Papa*, the Italian word for pope, simply means "father." Another even earlier name for this great god is Jano, and according to ancient tradition the guardian angel or higher self of a man in Latin countries was known as his "Jano" or "Genio." Similarly, the Female Pope represents Pope Joan, a legendary medieval woman who miraculously became pope. "Joan" is the anglicized version of the name Jana or Juno, the celestial goddess and consort of the All Father. The guardian spirit said to be set over the destiny of a woman was referred to as her "Juno."

In small tarot deals, the significator is generally put in a central position, with the other cards taking up their places around it, like satellites around a central sun. In larger deals, especially those requiring the entire complement of seventy-eight cards, the significator remains within the pack and is sought out as the marking point for the beginning of the divination.

Having selected your significator, your next task will be to address yourself to the problem of adequately mixing the cards. If you are performing the divination for yourself, you alone will be responsible for shuffling the deck. If you are reading the cards for someone else, both of you should take part in mixing them. Your object here is to introduce as much chance and randomization into the cards as possible. Theoretically, the ideal system is one which combines the maximum of mechanical rituals, such as rhythmical dealing and counting out, with the maximum of randomization through shuffling. You must fully permeate the cards with both your own and the querent's magnetism by this initial ritual, at the same time allowing "the gods" the fullest opportunity to intervene and arrange the cards to their dictates. One of the systems which accomplishes this best is probably the "forty-two," a method used by Italian witches that I shall discuss later. However, many practiced readers quite effectively dispense with all but the most perfunctory shuffle.

After the cards have been selected, they will be laid out in a pattern known as a spread or layout. There are a great many of these to choose from and some are better than others. Which method suits you best can be found out only by a process of trial and error, depending on how well you are able to cope with the cards themselves. The more suggestive the cards are for you, the more complex method you can use. However, if you are new to tarot I would strongly advise you to begin with one of the simpler layouts. Then if you find it fails to answer enough of your queries, move on to a more complex one. But don't start with the complicated ones. They will only confuse you and cause you to give up in despair.

It is best to memorize the various layouts so that you can

perform them without even thinking of where the cards should go. Don't worry about cards dropping or being misdealt, although your querent probably will assume that any "mistake" made will change his reading for the worse. Your main concern at this point should be to maintain the correct dreamy state of mind and to not consciously place known cards in known positions. Let the cards fall or spill as they will, but carry on regardless. Your attitude must be one of "the gods are guiding my hands." Some diviners even use the upset cards as a basis for a subsequent reading. You would be surprised how casual and simple a divination by a tarot master can appear to the uninitiated. The famous nineteenth-century cartomancer Marie-Anne Adelaide Lenormand, much in demand at the French court owing to the uncanny accuracy of her predictions, was said simply to have cut the cards to produce a reading for clients.

While on the subject of shuffling the deck, it would be as well to return briefly to the topic of "reversed" cards. According to many present-day diviners, a "reversed" upside-down card may connote the worst side of the image's character, analogous to a "retrograde" planet in astrology. The reading of a separate meaning for a reversed card consequently doubles the available single interpretations of the tarots—theoretically, instead of 78 variables, you would be dealing with 156. This notion of reversal only came into tarot interpretation with the advent of the cabalist school in France, along with its theosophical speculations of *Diabolus est Deus Inversus* ("the Devil is the mirror image of god"). According to medieval traditions the cards meant the same whether reversed or dealt the right way up.* From a practical point of view, the complexity involved in shuffling the cards to ensure definite reversals, the subsequent deal (Do you flip the cards over when you deal them? Should they be counted as reversed according to the position of the querent or the diviner? How do you tell whether the pip cards are reversed or not?) can become very complicated for a beginner.

*See *Le Ingeniose Sorte,* Venice, Marcolino, 1550.

If you feel that the more modern method of interpreting reversed cards negatively won't floor you, then go ahead and use it. Most people do. The cards must speak to you personally, and your own intuition must be the last arbiter as to which method you adopt. Cartomantic rules are only rule-of-thumb guidelines which have been evolved over the years.

A good way of accomplishing such card reversals simply is to make a random "pool" of the deck face downward on the table after the initial shuffle and cut. The cards should be stirred around by the querent and then single cards drawn one by one and handed to the reader with one end or the other pointing toward him. On receiving the card, the reader should take care in turning it face up to preserve its orientation exactly, reversed or right way up, before positioning it on the layout.

According to the traditional meanings attributed to the cards, we saw that not all reversals are bad. A reversed bad card may undo its harm! It becomes a "negated negative." But one last word of caution: Whether you choose to regard reversals as bad omens or not, remember the cards are not, and never will be, mechanical counters which will dial you out an answer to your problems like a computer. They are simply stimuli to start your own powers of ESP and intuition flowing.

Once the cards have been well shuffled to the satisfaction of the reader and querent alike, the traditional termination of the process is performed by means of a triple cut made with the querent's left hand. The cards should be divided into two heaps, a larger and a smaller, and the larger of the heaps divided again into two heaps, roughly equal in size. The three heaps are then restacked, again with the left hand, in any order the querent wishes. We are now ready for the layout.

Tarot layouts

Basically there are two types of tarot layouts: those which follow a preset pattern and those which don't. The first I shall categorize as divining "with a framework," the second as "without a framework."

Working with a preset framework is by far the easiest method for a beginner, although as you grow more adept you may be inclined to discard such devices and work solely intuitively, using the entire deck and waiting for the appropriate cards to pop out at you from the array—to seize your attention of their own accord during a reading. But this really is advanced work, and there is nothing ignominious in relying on a framework, however practiced a diviner you may be.

The framework or pattern that the cards are dealt out in may best be compared to the mandalas of Indian mysticism. Parts of the pattern will refer to different things like past, future, hopes and fears. Serious tarot readers will often employ a special tabletop or cloth to deal the cards on. These are occasionally painted or embroidered with a design composed of a combination of the various frameworks they intend to use. If a cloth is used, black silk is frequently chosen, traditionally regarded as a good insulator from magical vibrations and thus providing a protected area into which the cards can be dealt—an idea having much in common with that of the sorcerer's magical circle. The designs of these cloths vary from person to person. A diviner may well employ one embroidered with a hexagram (a six-pointed Star of David) a circular, twelve-house horoscope chart, a large equal-armed cross symbolizing the potent tetragram, or simply a triangle circumscribed by a circle. Cards dealt on the latter are sometimes referred to as being dealt "in trinity." When not in use, the cards themselves are often wrapped in the silk cloth to protect them from contaminating vibrations.

The Simple Draw

Apart from merely cutting the pack at random, the simplest layout is a gypsy method involving three cards: the significator —already selected—and two others which the querent draws at random from the deck (without looking at them beforehand, of course). (See Figure 6.) The first of these traditionally represents the querent himself; the second, a situation or person he is about to encounter.

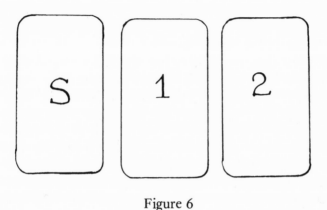

Figure 6

Before interpreting the cards drawn, the gypsy custom is to demand token payment by "crossing the palm" of the diviner with silver. Some have said this practice is a remnant of the ancient rite of offering silver to the priests of Hermes, the god of divination. As we shall see later, the trickster god plays a great part in the symbolism of the Major Arcana.

This layout may be elaborated upon by the addition of a third card. In this instance the first card drawn will act as an indicator of the past, the second the present, and the third the future. Remember, especially in the case of these elementary divinations, the cards must be allowed to suggest the answer rather than be rigidly interpreted. If you have done your homework on them, this won't be difficult.

The Grand Cross

Building numerically from the simple draw method, we come to the "Grand Cross." Referred to by Waite under the name of a Celtic method, it is, like the Simple Draw, much in use among tarot readers. (See Figure 7.)

The significator is placed centrally and an unseen card is drawn by the querent from the deck and set on top of it. This represents the querent's present state of mind and is said to "cover" him. The second card drawn is laid crosswise on top of this and represents any obstacles he is confronting at the moment, being said to "cross" him.

The third card is placed below the first two and represents what is "beneath" the querent—namely, those ideas which were once part of his thinking but have now been relegated to the background. The fourth card is placed above the significator, being said to "crown" the querent. This is an indicator of his present hopes or fears. The fifth card is placed according to which direction the gaze of the significator is turned in. If its gaze is to the right, then the fifth card is placed on the left, and vice versa; it represents the factors passing out of the question, "that which is behind him." Should the significator not face in either direction but be presented full face, then assume the left-hand side to represent the past, as in your Simple Draw method. Similarly, the direction in which the gaze of the significator is turned represents "that which is before him," the future, and this is where the sixth card is laid. Should the significator face front, then this will be the right-hand side.

You have now constructed the basic cross. Some readers use only the Major Arcana for this divination instead of the full deck of seventy-eight cards. The twenty-one (minus the significator) or twenty-two (if you plan to use a court card) should be shuffled and cut by the querent in the usual manner and then reshuffled by the diviner, and a number between one and twenty-one, or twenty-two (if you are using a court card) selected at random by the querent. The number selected is then counted off in cards from the top of the deck and the card arrived upon placed in position on the significator. The process then continues as before, with random numbers being selected from between one and twenty on the second card, one and nineteen on the third, and so on.

Four additional cards are sometimes selected to represent the future condition of the querent (number seven), his future home life (number eight), his future hopes or fears (number nine) and, lastly, the final outcome, if it be a problem that has been inquired about (ten).

Figure 7

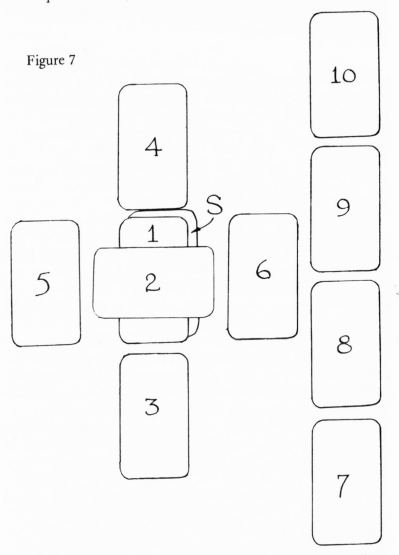

Alternatively, when forming a Grand Cross you may continue the deal after covering and crossing the significator by placing one card on the right, "spring," one at the base, "summer," one on the left, "autumn" and, finally, one above, "winter," thus deriving a reading applicable to a yearly cycle. The so-called Horoscope deal, to be described below, can also be employed to a similar end.

The Hexagram deal

A deal involving a circle of six cards plus the significator at

Figure 8

the center offers a slightly more elaborate version of the Simple Draw method. (See Figure 8.)

Here the cards are dealt clockwise as selected, beginning at the top and concluding at the top left-hand corner. The cards in the ascending triangle may be read as influences working in favor of the querent, while those of the descending, inverted triangle are working against him. This is a good framework for a reading concerned specifically with a question, as opposed to a general reading.

Restricted deck deals

When you are seeking enlightenment on one specific problem, a traditional method of narrowing down the range of variables is to divine with a restricted deck using one of the simpler layouts, such as the Simple Draw, Grand Cross or Hexagram. A restricted deck simply means using one or two suits germane to the problem, either with or without the Major Arcana, depending on how deeply seated the problem is. If the query is a superficial one, leave the Major Arcana out also. Thus, for a specific answer to a question concerning a business transaction, use the combined suits of Coins and Swords and Rods; for a purely financial one, Coins only; an emotional one, Cups, probably with the addition of the Major Arcana. A problem of work, especially if it is concerned with artistry in any form, might call for Rods and Cups, again with the Major Arcana added in.

The Planetary deal

Here we use seven cards dealt in a seven-pointed star in the sequence shown (Figure 9). Each of the seven points is taken to represent the traditional field of influence of one of the astrological planets—the Moon, Mercury, Venus, the Sun, Mars, Jupiter and Saturn—and the cards are read to represent the influences working in these fields.

1. Place of the Moon—matters of the home
2. Place of Mercury—matters of business, skill or deceit
3. Place of Venus—the love life
4. Place of the Sun—matters concerned with fame or achievement
5. Place of Mars—matters of enmity or adversity
6. Place of Jupiter—matters of gain, acquisition and expansion
7. Place of Saturn—matters of intellectual deliberation and general restriction

The cards should be paired and read in juxtaposition: that of

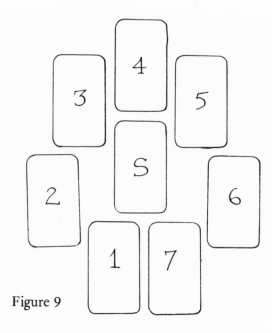

Figure 9

the Moon contrasted to that of the Sun; Venus to Mars; Jupiter to Saturn. When a seemingly irreconcilable problem is encountered, the solution will be found to lie in the card of Mercury, the reconciler.

Alternatively, the seven cards may be read to give a projected weekly review. In this instance each card should be interpreted individually. You should also make up your mind *before* you begin the deal which type of reading you intend to use. The card readings in this instance are:

Place 4—Sunday
1—Monday
5—Tuesday
2—Wednesday
6—Thursday
3—Friday
7—Saturday

The Horoscope spread

The significator again is placed centrally and the cards selected positioned around the circle in the order indicated (see Figure 10). This pattern will, of course, be familiar to students of astrology. It is none other than a chart of the twelve zodiacal "houses" that the sky is divided into by astrologers. Each division, or house, governs a specific area of human experience, similar to those of the planetary places in the previous layout.

House 1—the personality of the querent
      2—his financial affairs
      3—travel and communication
      4—his home life and parents
      5—his pleasures
      6—his health
      7—marriage or partnerships
      8—legalities or deaths
      9—his philosophy or religion
    10—his business career
    11—his friends
    12—his burdens, restrictions and secret fears

For a more specialized horoscope reading the significator is left in and the entire pack of seventy-eight is distributed around and around the circle counterclockwise, building up the packets of cards in the twelve houses to packets of six or seven. The packet containing the significator is then removed and the other eleven heaps discarded. Noting the house and the special field of interest which it represents, the packet should be spread out left to right and read *in the direction in which the significator is facing*. When a series of cards is to be read, this is always the practice to be adopted. So when a significator makes its appearance reversed, far from indicating some dire influence emanating from an occult source, it simply means that the cards should be read in the opposite direction to the spread in which the significator appears right side up. Should the significator lead the line of cards, there being in fact *none* before him, then

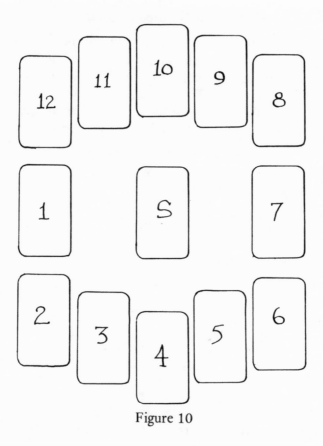

Figure 10

the reading in question is null and void and should be repeated using a different spread and, if possible, rephrasing the question if there is one.

The Tree of Life spread

This is a more complex cabalistic variant of the Planetary spread and lays the entire pack out in the pattern of the tree of life glyph. (See p.85 for a discussion of the philosophy behind this symbol.) The order of dealing is thus (see Figure 11):

Card 1, 11, 21, 41, 61, 71   Kether—inner spiritual quest

Card 2, 12, 22, 32, 42, 52,   Chokmah—personal initiative
    62, 72
Card 3, 13, 23, etc.   Binah—sorrows and burdens
Card 4, 14, 24, etc.   Gedulah—financial gains
Card 5, 15, 25, etc.   Geburah—enemies and discords
Card 6, 16, etc.   Tiphareth—glory and fame
Card 7, 17, etc.   Netzach—love
Card 8, 18, etc.   Hod—wheeling   and   dealing;
                                  communication
Card 9, 19, etc.   Yesod—health
Card 10, 20, etc.   Malkuth—the home

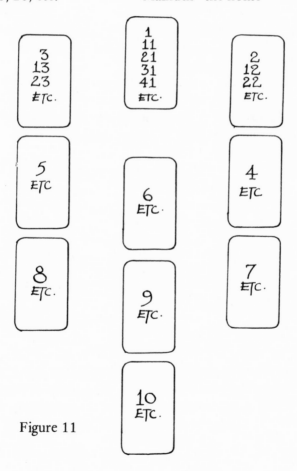

Figure 11

Again, all cards except the heap containing the significator are discarded, the dominant theme of the significator's sphere noted (the home, health, etc.) and the accompanying cards laid out left to right and read off in the direction of the significator's gaze.

Twenty-one-Card layouts

Here are three methods of divining using twenty-one cards. First, a simple traditional gypsy method.

Method I

Having selected your significator and shuffled and cut in the correct manner, let the querent select twenty-one cards at random from the unseen pack.

Distribute them in a semicircle from left to right (see Figure 12).

The first three cards on the left-hand side are said to represent the querent's personality, specifically his present psychological condition.

The next three are said to stand for his present home life.

Figure 12

Cards seven, eight and nine show his present desires.

Ten, eleven and twelve indicate his expectations.

Thirteen, fourteen and fifteen show what he does *not* expect.

Sixteen, seventeen and eighteen show his immediate future, while nineteen, twenty and twenty-one show more long-term influences.

Before actually committing himself to words—and this applies to all readings—the diviner should study the cards first to get the overall feel of them. Remember, they have to read as a unit, one card influencing and often totally changing the implications of another.

Methods II and III

These are best used for answering a specific question. Both require the entire pack of seventy-eight cards. After shuffling and cutting, these should either be laid out on the floor in a huge circle in which you and the querent place yourselves or arranged on a table in six rows of thirteen. Method II requires that you find the preselected significator and then, moving in the direction indicated by the card's gaze (or left in the case of the Female Pope, right for the Pope), read every seventh card until twenty-one have been accounted for (twenty-two including the significator). If you have arranged the cards in rows, be sure that you get the order right when you start your progression. For this reason, although cumbersome, the floor circle method is better here. When you come to the end of the deck, return to the beginning and continue your counting, until the full complement of twenty-one has been read.

Method III relies on the same layout but also on the use of two dice which are shaken and cast by the querent. The sum of the two faces indicates the number of cards to be counted along. Again the reading is complete when twenty-one cards have been counted out.

In both of these methods it is helpful if the diviner removes the cards as they are arrived at and places them in a small circle away from the bulk of the others for closer scrutiny.

Figure 13

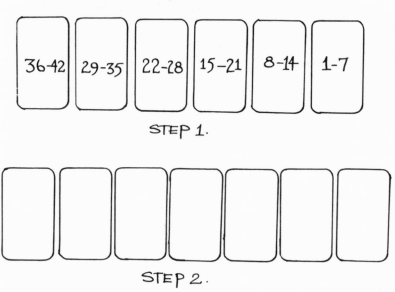

STEP 1.

STEP 2.

Of course, both methods may be considerably simplified by just counting off the required cards from the upward facing pack. This detracts from the ritual, however, which I find is an integral part of the process.

Finally, we should consider the area of the more complex tarot spreads. Until you have got the knack of "sliding over" the cards with ease to produce a reading, my advice is that you stay with the simpler variants. The complex ones are for experts. However, as it is quite probable that some of the readers will want to pursue the subject to more advanced levels, here are four of the major layouts.

The Forty-two-Card spread

This is a method at one time chiefly used by Italian witches, subsequently becoming popular in France (see Figure 13).

Step 1. After you have prepared the cards in your usual

manner, the querent should select forty-two cards at random from the deck and form a line of six heaps, seven cards to each, *right to left*, face upward. Selected cards one to seven should be contained in the first heap on the right; eight to fourteen in the next, and so on.

Step 2. Having done this, take up the first heap on the right and lay it out, right to left. Take up the second heap and also deal it out right to left on top of the cards from the first heap. Repeat this procedure until the six seven-card heaps are exhausted and you are now confronted by seven six-card heaps.

Step 3. Skim off the top card of each heap, shuffling them together and laying them out, right to left, as always, in a new line.

Step 4. Take the next two cards from each heap, shuffle them and lay them out as two new lines under the first.

Step 5. Gather up the remaining twenty-one cards, shuffle them and lay them out in three lines beneath your first three. Again, you are confronted by six lines of seven cards.

Step 6. Search for the significator—in this instance the Pope (Hierophant) for a male querent, the Female Pope (High Priestess) for a woman. If it appears within the spread, simply remove it and place it to the left-hand side of the array if it is the Female Pope, the right-hand side if the Pope. The querent should then draw another card unseen from the remaining pack to fill the gap. If the significator does not appear on the table, then simply search the unused deck for it and place it accordingly.

Step 7. Read the cards beginning at the top right-hand corner, working right to left, and ending at the bottom left-hand corner.

As you will notice, this process uses no framework. There is no division of the pattern into convenient areas of interpretation, such as "past" and "future." It offers very little support for the conscious reasoning processes to get to work on and because of this may be reckoned one of the more advanced methods. It is, however, to be recommended for its repetitious

STEPS 3,4 AND 5

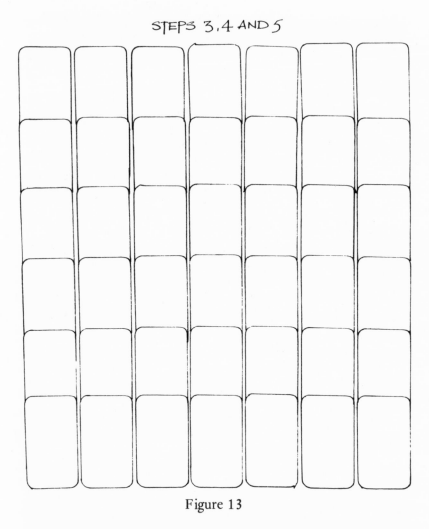

Figure 13

ritual and enormous attention to randomization. Fate is allowed every opportunity to step in and take a hand.

Another process which employs a good ritual is:

The Horseshoe spread (See Figures 14)

Step 1. Having shuffled the entire deck of seventy-eight and

Figure 14

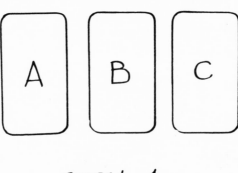

STEPS 1-4

performed the triple cut, deal them into three heaps, A, B and C, of twenty-six cards each.

Step 2. Heap B should be taken and placed off to the right. Heaps A and C should then be gathered together and shuffled by the querent.

Step 3. The shuffled cards of A and C should again be dealt out into three heaps of seventeen cards, A, B and C, and the remaining single card placed off to the *left*.

Step 4. Again remove the central heap, B, and place it off to the right alongside the other B pile. Shuffle A and C together with the single remainder card of the previous deal.

Step 5. Deal these cards into three heaps of eleven cards each. Again remove the flanking heaps A and C and discard them along with the remaining two cards left over from the deal. Now turn your attention to the three remaining B heaps off on your right. Pick up the heap you made first, containing twenty-six cards. Lay it out in a large horseshoe shape arching away from you, placing the first card in the bottom right-hand corner and the last in the bottom left-hand corner.

Then, beginning with the first card laid down and ending on the last, make your reading, which traditionally is said to refer to the psychological condition of the querent in the near future.

Having dispensed with the twenty-six cards, remove them and lay out the heap containing seventeen in exactly the same manner.

The area referred to by these cards is traditionally that of the querent's work or occupation and his thoughts about it, again in the immediate future.

The last pile of eleven cards when laid out is said to refer specifically to the querent's coming material condition—namely, his health, monetary situation and home life.

Thus the three horseshoes may be said to represent the spiritual, intellectual and material aspects of the querent's future.

"Le Grand Jeu" and "the Triangle" are the last two spreads I shall deal with. They represent the most complex type of tarot divination you can perform.

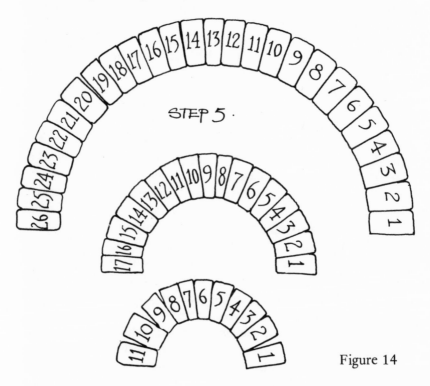

Figure 14

Le Grand Jeu uses sixty-six cards, whereas the Triangle employs the whole deck. If you think the preceding systems were mind-boggling, just take a look at these!

Le Grand Jeu

After selecting the significator, placing it centrally and shuffling and cutting the deck, let the querent draw sixty-six cards one after another, unseen, of course. These should be placed face upward according to the following layout (Figure 15):

Cards 1 through 11 in a column down the right-hand side of the table, beginning at the top.

Cards 12 through 22 up the left-hand side in a column, leaving plenty of room in between.

Cards 23 through 33 right to left along the top of the table, joining the two columns like a beam.

Now, beginning halfway between the two side pillars on the remaining unfilled side of your square of tarots, lay cards 34 through 66, containing the significator, in a counterclockwise circle within these boundaries. Leave gaps in your circle between cards 44 and 45, between 55 and 56, and between 66 and 34 (where the two ends of the circle join).

Finally, place the remaining 11 cards below the significator in center circle. They will not be read.

Your spread is now complete.

Cards 1 through 11 and 34 through 44 are traditionally said to refer to what has passed apropos the querent.

Cards 23 through 33 and 45 through 55 represent the present.

Cards 12 through 22 and 56 through 66 represent what is yet to come for the querent.

As you can see, there are a great many cards to deal with here, and unless you have already acquired the knack of letting the cards "drift together," the best you will achieve as a reading is a very muddled hotchpotch of ideas and feelings.

Work up to this method. Don't attempt it to begin with,

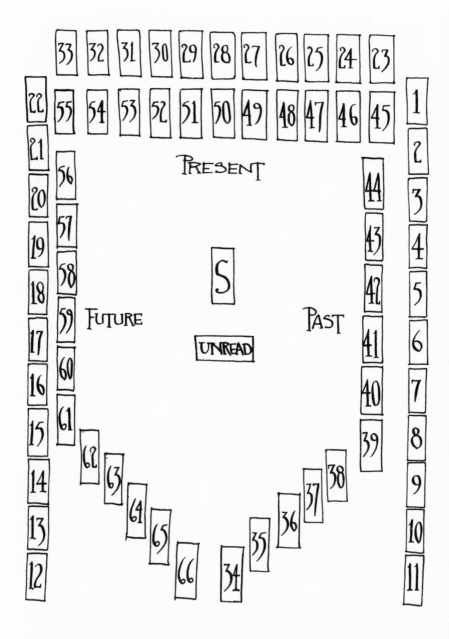

Figure 15

because you will probably only be discouraged by the psychic indigestion it will cause. Your deep mind has to be led to the point where it can pick out and enlarge upon the relevant tarot symbols, and this usually requires practice with the simpler spreads to begin with. The more card variables you place in your tarot layout, the more accurate and developed your intuition has to be.

The Triangle

This method is simply a convenient way of arranging the entire deck of seventy-eight cards for the most complex type of divination, one with no physical selection of cards or convenient division into past, present and future. As such it is really more in the nature of a tarot meditation.

After selecting the significator and placing it at the bottom left- or right-hand corner of where your triangle will be (left for the Pope, right for the High Priestess), the cards should be shuffled and cut in the usual manner. The querent should then draw random cards until the entire deck is exhausted. These should be placed in a line leading from the significator to the left for a female querent, right for a male.

When twelve (including the significator) have been lined up, the thirteenth should be placed above and just between cards eleven and twelve to begin another line leading back on its tracks above the first, which has now become the base of the triangle.

This second line contains only eleven cards, and on reaching card number twenty-three again jumps up a rung to make the next zigzag layer back on its tracks. (See Figure 16.)

Thus a complete triangle is built up containing the entire deck of seventy-eight tarot cards. The last card remaining in the querent's hand represents the resolution of the divination and is placed at the apex of the triangle. The cards are then read beginning at the significator and working up to the apex, always following the same direction that the cards were laid in.

This layout represents the entire cosmic tarot ladder, and it requires the fully awakened intuition of the tarot adept to

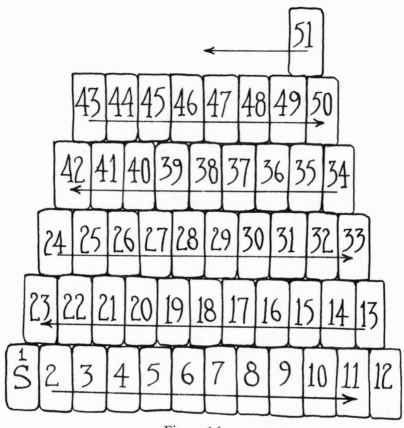

Figure 16

climb it. Only by means of a complete and unobstructed inter-relating between his deep and everyday minds can this serpentine path be followed with any degree of assurance, with the cards marshaled behind the significator coming to life and assuming meaningful patterns to the eye of the perceptive reader.

Two tarot games

Tarot Pelmanism

The simplest game for familiarizing yourself with the cards is that of "Pelmanism." The entire pack is laid out face down at random, and players take turns at turning over two cards for general inspection and then reversing them again. The object of the game is to make pairs. When a pair—such as two knights or two fours—are turned up, the player responsible removes them, scoring them as a "trick." Any Major Arcana trump pairs with any other trump. Play continues until all the cards have been collected. The winner is the player who has collected the most tricks. The practice of declaring out loud the name of the cards turned over is a good one to adopt; it will be found to aid the memorization process.

The game of Trumps

Though devised during the Middle Ages, "Trumps," or "Triumphs," is still played in Europe to this day. It is really very easy, especially for the card enthusiast, once you get the knack of the point counts. The object of the game is like that of bridge: to reach a score of 100. This is achieved in two ways: by making "melds," which means counting up significant cards and sequences in your hand before play begins; and by scoring up points in your various tricks during the play itself.

SCORING

Any 10-card sequence in trumps or any of the four Minor Arcana suits—15 points
Any 7-card sequence in trumps or any of the four Minor Arcana suits—10
Any 4-card sequence in trumps or any of the four Minor Arcana suits—5
Any three of the following trumps:
  King of Swords
  King of Rods
  King of Cups

King of Coins   15 points
Juggler
Fool
World

(If you have only two of these before the declaration of melds, you may ask either of the other players for a third tarot trump. If none has one, you score 5 points. If someone does, you must take it but score *zero*; you must then give him a discard from your hand in return.)

To continue with the meld scores:

All five "lesser trumps" (Juggler, Female Pope, Empress, Emperor, Pope)—15 points

Four lesser trumps—10

Three lesser trumps—5

All five "greater trumps" (Star, Moon, Sun, Judgment, World)—15

Four greater trumps—10

Three greater trumps—5

Ten trumps (any order)—10

Thirteen trumps (any order)—15

TRICK SCORES

As the game is played out after meld declaration, points are scored by trick takers, only the highest card in the trick being counted.

Tricks taken by:

A tarot trump (any king, the Juggler or the World—not the Fool)—5 points

Any queen—4

Any knight—3

Any page—2

Any other card—1

A very important point to remember here is that for the *masculine* suits—Rods and Swords—after the regular order of precedence from king to page, the ten ranks highest and the ace lowest. For the *feminine* suits—Cups and Coins—the pip card order is reversed, ace being high and ten low. Thus in the suit of Cups, for instance, the page of Cups will beat the ace of Cups, the ace of Cups will beat the nine of Cups and the nine, the ten. In the suit of Swords, on the other hand, the two will beat the ace.

THE GAME

Ideally three should play, but if only two are available, a third hand should be dealt as a dummy and left unseen, keeping both players guessing what cards are out.

Deal should be cut for. For the sake of simplicity during the cut, count aces low, kings high, trumps highest of all (except for the Fool which, as always, counts zero). If the same cards of different suits are cut, such as nine of Cups and nine of Rods, repeat the cutting.

After shuffling the cards well, deal twenty-five cards to each hand, beginning at the dealer's right and going counterclockwise, five at a time (this helps to influence the odds in favor of sequences showing up in the hands). The remaining three cards are then placed at the dealer's right hand as the pot, or "widow," as it is known in Europe. Alternatively, for a harder game you may deal twenty-four cards to each player one at a time and place the remaining six cards in the widow.

All players should now sort their hands into the various sequences and melds. Cards may do double work. For instance, a king could figure in a tarot trump count as well as a sequence. Likewise, the Juggler might be used in a tarot trump count as well as in a lesser trump one.

Once you have sorted out which cards will be useful to you, the dealer may discard up to six of his useless cards and exchange them for those in the widow. However, he must discard his own *before* picking up the hidden ones. He need not exchange the full amount of six—just as many as he feels he needs. If he chooses not to exchange any, or only one or two, the option then passes to the player on the dealer's right. He in turn may then exchange discards of his own for the cards remaining. Should there still remain a card or two, the third player (if there is one) receives the option to exchange one or two of his own for these.

It is during this initial phase of the game that tarot trump requests should be made.

When you have finished discarding and requesting, the various melds and sequences should be declared, exhibited and scored, beginning with the player to the right of the dealer and traveling counterclockwise.

Once you have a chance to see what cards are held by the other player or players, you can plan your strategy of play accordingly.

Having noted down the various scores, each player picks up his cards again, re-sorts them into suits, and play begins.

Second hand leads again. All players must either follow suit or trump. The only time a nonsuit nontrump discard is allowed is when the player in question has no trumps or correct suit cards to follow with. The only exception to this rule is when the player possesses the Fool, whose only use, characteristically, is that of a scapegoat or sacrifice. If you have a high card, such as a king or the Juggler, that you don't want to have snapped up by the third hand or because the king is the last card you possess of the suit led, you may play the Fool as a substitute. The poor Fool has no number and is in fact the lowest card in the deck. If he is led, any other card can take him. (We shall see where this traditional attribute of total vulnerability comes from later on.)

Continue counterclockwise with the taker of the trick leading until all the cards are exhausted, scoring as you play. Only one scoring card may be counted per trick. For instance, if a trick contained a page, a queen and a king, the person who played the king scores only the king—5 points.

When you have finished the hand, make a total of each player's meld and trick scores. If there are three players, the *lowest* scorer forfeits his entire score. The second highest scorer *subtracts* his score from the highest and likewise scores nothing. Only the highest scorer achieves a final score, which is what is left after the second highest has subtracted his score.

For instance, if player A scores 30 points, B 20 and C 40, then B forfeits his entire score, leaving him a count of zero, and A likewise scores zero. C only scores 10 points (40 minus 30).

If only two persons play, then the lesser score is simply subtracted from the greater. The first player to reach 100 points is the winner.

Deal should pass to the right at each new hand, thus giving each player the advantage of first crack at the widow and her dowry.

The actual scoring can be accomplished with a cribbage board if two play, a bezique marker or pencil and paper for three.

CHAPTER 2

Where Did the Tarot Come From?

The first appearance of recognizable tarot cards in Europe can be traced to A.D. 1392. An entry was made at that time in the ledger of the court treasury of King Charles VI of France to the effect that a specified sum of money had been paid to a painter, Jacquemin Gringoneur, in return for three packs of cards. These cards had been designed especially for the amusement of the king " . . . in gold and diverse colors, ornamented with many devices . . . ."

Seventeen of these cards are all that remain of those packs. They may be seen in the Bibliothèque Nationale in Paris, mysterious and exquisite miniatures painted on vellum, illuminated with gold leaf and exotic pigments like ground lapis lazuli, "dragon's blood" and mummy dust, in the style of the day.

Whether the cards were invented by Gringoneur or merely copied by him from packs already in existence is a matter of conjecture. No evidence of substance has been documented to indicate that they originated earlier, though there are a lot of suggestive clues. Many of these clues have been formulated into theories, but they remain theories only.

One theory places their origin in China, where playing cards were definitely in use before the eleventh century A.D., some three hundred years before the packs of King Charles VI. A Chinese playing card at present in the Staatliches Museum für Volkerkunde in Berlin is probably the oldest of these. It depicts a little figure of a man with a symbol denoting a specific sum of money over his head, which may indicate that it was used in gambling.

Another theory holds that tarot was introduced into Europe from India by bands of wandering gypsies. The Romany language is now known to be a remarkably pure dialect of Sanskrit, the language of sacred Hindu writings and the oldest of the Indo-European tongues. The word "tarot" may well derive from the Hungarian gypsy word *tar*, meaning "a deck of cards," which in turn derives from the Sanskrit *taru*.

The third theory of the tarot's origin also connects the pack with gypsies but this time assumes that the Romany bands came from Egypt. In this case, of course, the deck they brought with them would have come from the land of Khem.

This theory seems more valid when one considers the evidence. The word "gypsy" itself is an old English abbreviation of "Egyptian," although this may only mean that the ignorant English merely fancied that the strange, dark-haired nomads had emigrated from Egypt. On the other hand, the crypt of the Church of Les Saintes Maries de la Mer in the Camargue area of southern France is reserved exclusively to the gypsies, even to this day. It contains the shrine of Saint Sara of Egypt, supposedly their patron saint. Since Sara is somewhat suspect as a Catholic saint, she may turn out to be none other than Sarapis, the Egyptian god of the dead, in his mortuary crypt. In the Camargue there is a dark tradition that the shrine of Sara rests upon an ancient altar dedicated to Mithras, the Persian sun god. It is interesting to note that the Egyptian deity Sarapis was assimilated into the Mithraic pantheon. Yet none of this can be called proof of origin.

Both the Chinese and Indian notions are fine as theories. However, when one actually compares a deck of tarot cards with an Indian or Chinese card game, one will find very little symbolism in common, particularly where the all-important

Major Arcana is concerned. Any similarity is limited to the fifty-six cards of the Minor Arcana. This is one of the arguments advanced in favor of the original independence of the major and minor sequences. It is certainly possible that the four tarot suits refer to the four castes of Hinduism: the cup to the priests or Brahmans, the sword to the warrior overlords or Kshatriyas, the coin to the merchants or Vaisyas, and the baton to the serfs or Sudras.

The Major Arcana obviously shares a lot of symbolism with the metaphysical teachings of India, notably Buddhism, whose founder, Gautama, is thought to have been born some 560 years before Christ. The Fool might well be said to represent the wandering monk, or Sannyasin himself; the Emperor and Empress Suddhodana, King of the Sakyas, and his bride Maya Devi, Buddha's parents; the chariot, the juggernaut or triumphal car of Vishnu; the Pope, the Hermit, the Hanged Man and Death the Man of Religion, Ancient, Cripple and Corpse said to have been encountered by Buddha prior to his enlightenment; the Wheel of Fortune quite obviously the Wheel of Rebirth and Karma; the Devil Yama, the bull-headed god of death; the World Mount Meru surrounded by the four Dhyani Buddhas; and so on. Undoubtedly the tarot deals with the same ideas but filtered through an almost entirely Western doctrinal mesh.

The last of these three theories—the Egyptian—is the oldest. It was evolved by eighteenth-century occultists who had rediscovered the tarot, recognizing that there was something about these quaint old cards that rendered them considerably more important than mere fortune-telling devices. Because in a sense this third theory forms a part of tarot history, we shall consider it in its proper sequence presently. Before we do, let us examine the religious climate that prevailed in the fourteenth century when the tarot first made its appearance in Europe.

Christianity officially reigned supreme in Europe, though beneath the surface paganism still lurked in many fairly obvious forms, resulting in terrible ecclesiastical persecution of heretics.

The church pursued its own ends with a zeal compounded by fanatical piety and simple political opportunism. During the twelfth and thirteenth centuries unorthodox Christian sects like the Waldenses, Cathari, Albigenses and Bogomils were ruthlessly harried by the papacy, with fire and sword. The monastic order of the Knights Templar also fell under the papal eye of displeasure during the fourteenth century for similar reasons and was systematically burned out of Christendom's body like a malignant wart. The Holy Inquisition arranged an equal settlement of the confiscated property of the disinherited Templars between themselves and the crown of France.

Many of the doctrines preached by these heretical Christian sects were drawn from late pagan religions that flourished well into the fourth century. Today these are grouped together under the collective title of "Gnosticism." Most of the pagan rituals appropriated by the Roman and unorthodox churches for their rites also came from these cults. The word "gnostic" itself is derived from the Greek and implies much the same as the Anglo-Saxon words "wizard" or "witch"—that is, "someone who knows," a wise man or initiate. Stemming as it did from the eastern provinces of the Roman Empire, Gnosticism mixed together Indian, Chaldean, Persian and Egyptian magical doctrines and seasoned them with Greek philosophy and Hebrew cabalistic beliefs. Alexandria became the center for Gnostic learning around the second century A.D., and Coptic Christianity absorbed many of the old Gnostic symbols dating from that period. In this manner the Egyptian ankh, or *crux Ansata*— that occult symbol so popular today among the "love generation"—passed from the ancient Egyptian papyri into North African Christianity as an alternative to the cross of crucifixion. (See Figure 17.) Similarly, it is from this welter of Gnostic cults that the occult arts of the West appear to derive: alchemy, astrology and, indeed, the images of the tarot cards themselves.

How did this Gnostic lore survive in the face of the considerable effort made on the part of Christianity to stamp it out? The answer is an interesting one, and it leads us directly to our tarot trail. Gnosticism was preserved within the fold of the church itself, admittedly but understandably in an altered form. While without the cloister walls—the only places of learning to

Figure 17

survive during the Dark Ages—all those guilty of well worship, tree worship and any other pagan practices were being pressured into Christian conformity, within those sanctified walls the older doctrines were preserved and studied, albeit under a mask of science and learning consonant with ecclesiastic respectability. The planetary and stellar gods of old, after their brief period of residence within the port of Gnosticism, found a more permanent haven in the twin sciences of astrology and alchemy. Many of the ancient deities fared worse, however, being transformed into demons in the Christian hierarchy of hell, their mangled names and descriptions being listed in Gnostically derived *grimoires*, such as the *Greater Key of Solomon,* the *Lesser Key of Solomon*, and the *Picatrix*, forbidden spell-books used to conjure up spirits and force them to do the operator's will. The monastic libraries often possessed copies of these conjuring books. In order to counter Satan's wiles, one must know the type of creature one is dealing with.

The occult principle behind a deck of tarot cards may also owe a lot to monasticism, if not for originating it, then at least for preserving it. Memory served a far greater purpose for the medieval monk than it does for us nowadays. All books then consisted of laboriously hand-written manuscripts. Indeed, the art of writing itself was hard to acquire. In view of this, vast tracts were often committed to memory. Memory or "mnemonic" systems similar to those so widely advertised today were very much in demand.

The most simple type of mnemonic system consists of a series of pictorial images, usually arranged in some special order, which may be used as a mental filing index or pigeonhole rack. The medieval student monk could, by vividly visualizing each portion of the tract he wished to learn, file the section away in one of his memory boxes until he needed to take the tract out of mental storage and look at it again. All that would be needed then was a return to the correct category image in order to release the associated portions. A similar type of memory system, using plants and trees and the digits of the hand as category images seems to have been used by druids and bards long before their Christian successors, the Dominican and Franciscan monks.*

The pigeonhole images themselves sometimes consisted of places or large buildings well known to the memorizer, and as he was usually a monk, these were often churches or abbeys. Pagan elements did creep in, though, especially since candidates for memory training were advised to make their own pictorial filing systems, and classical works like those of Virgil were not unknown, albeit often in a very garbled form.

In such a way the medieval *ars memorativa* or mnemotechnic was devised, which in many respects closely paralleled earlier classical systems of memory training used by orators, such as that of Metrodorus of Scepsis. Interestingly enough, investigations carried out by Professor Aleksandr Luria of Moscow University into the mental processes of a world-famous theatrical mnemonist of the 1920's revealed that the subject used similar, naturally evolved memorization techniques. In this instance, however, the mnemonist's imagery was completely self-devised. The items for memorization were "coded" into pictorial symbols, and the symbols were then arranged in their correct order along a visualized "route," such as the walk between a

*See Robert Graves, *The White Goddess* (London, Faber & Faber, 1961), Chap. 10-14.

well-known public building and the subject's home. They were placed in juxtaposition to such obvious landmarks as doorways and lampposts. When the correct sequence was to be remembered, all that was necessary was that the route be mentally retraced and the various items read off.*

Such systems fitted themselves well to the memorization of religious articles of belief. (See Figure 18.) "The Stations of the Cross" is one practice that remains to this day among Roman Catholics. "Credo tapestries," illustrating the Nicene or shorter Apostles' creeds, were woven on this principle.

The medieval brethren, however, omitted one very special belief from their theory of mnemotechnic which was an integral part of the ancient bardic and classical varieties—in fact, one may almost say it was the main reason for indulging in such practices: The frequent use of a complex mnemotechnic system was believed to result in the enlivening or "potentiating" of the imagination, which in turn brought mysterious benefits to the user other than merely a splendid memory. Benefits so special, in fact, as to be deserving of the description "supernatural," as the Jesuits, with their "spiritual exercises" of their founder Ignatius of Loyola, also came to suspect several centuries later.

There are quite a number of medieval memory systems still preserved in treatise form to this day. The best known is that of Ramon Lull, the *Ars Memoria*. Another is that of Peter of Ravenna, entitled *Phoenix, sive artificiosa Memoria (Phoenix, or the Artificial Memory)*, printed at Venice in 1491. Here the route memory image advocated is that of a church known to the prospective mnemonist. He is advised to commit it to memory by walking around it several times.

The *Ars Notoria* was another memory manual, and it was severely condemned by no less an ecclesiastic than Thomas Aquinas. This work is more germane to us than the others, being a memory system which retained all its pagan magical attributes. Its authorship was fathered alternately upon the

*A. R. Luria, *The Mind of a Mnemonist*, translated from Russian by Lynn Solotaroff (New York, Discus Books, 1969).

Figure 18

Greek magician Apollonius of Tyana, or Solomon, the wizard-king of Israel. By meditating upon the magical notae—symbolic memory images and diagrams—and intoning magical formulas, the wizard sent a call ringing into the world of the unseen and stirred up supernatural agencies to his aid. Students of Eastern mysticism will discern here elements of yantra and mantra yoga. The memory images were planetary and zodiacal, and the grouping of associated images about them served a far deeper purpose than merely providing one with an infallible shopping list. It was from such a pagan sequence of images that the tarot deck itself appears to have evolved.

The divergence between the tarot as a deck of playing cards as opposed to a set of memory system notae did not emerge until the early fifteenth century. By 1423, notae used for gaming purposes must have been fairly widespread, for the evangelical monk Bernardino of Siena, in one of his fire-and-brimstone sermons, vehemently preached against them in Bologna as an invention of the devil. Historically speaking, the French deck of Charles VI was followed by that of the Venetian Visconti family in 1415. Others undoubtedly were produced in the interim, many perishing in the flames lit by Bernardino and his followers. The Charles VI and Visconti decks represent what today is regarded as the conventional tarot pack—a set of twenty-two trumps and fifty-six pip cards, making a deck of seventy-eight in all. Though Charles VI's trumps were unnumbered, the Italian fifteenth-century decks often possessed Roman numerals at the top of each card, indicating some sort of sequence. The order has been constantly switched around throughout the ages in various attempts to make the cards' meanings fit one theory or another. A fifteenth-century manuscript with a marginal note dealing with tarot cards gives us the following sequence* (beside them I have listed their usual titles):

    I   Il Bagatella (the Juggler)
   II   Imperatrice (the Empress)
  III   Imperator (the Emperor)
   IV   La papessa (the Female Pope)
    V   El papa (the Pope)
   VI   La tempetia (Temperantia?) (Temperance)
  VII   L'Amore (the Lovers)
 VIII   Le caro triumphale (the Chariot)
   IX   La Fortez (Strength)
    X   La rotta (the Wheel of Fortune)
   XI   El gobbo (the Hermit)
  XII   Lo impichato (the Hanged Man)
 XIII   La morte (Death)
  XIV   El diavolo (the Devil)
   XV   La sagitta (the Lightning-struck Tower)
  XVI   La stella (the Star)

*Sermones de Ludo cum Aliis (fifteenth-century illuminated manuscript in the collection of United States Playing Card Co., Cincinnati, Ohio).

XVII La luna (the Moon)
XVIII El sole (the Sun)
  XIX Lo angelo (Judgment)
  XX La justicia (Justice)
  XXI El mondo ave dio padre (the World)
XXII El mato.

The Italians also produced two other important kinds of tarot packs with differing numbers of cards. One was the "tarochinno," or "little tarot deck," from Bologna, containing all twenty-two trumps but lacking several of the minor cards, making only sixty-two cards instead of the original seventy-eight. It appeared first around 1415 and was probably the one Bernardino preached against. The second is common to Florence, of about the same period, and is known as the Minchiate. This contains ninety-eight cards in all, having in addition to those of the regular tarot pack cards representing the twelve signs of the zodiac, the four Aristotelian elements (earth, air, fire and water), and the four remaining virtues apparently left out of the seventy-eight, namely prudence, faith, hope and charity. This is undoubtedly the pack that is used in the Florentine witch-spell mentioned by C. G. Leland and quoted at the beginning of this book: The deck has to be laid out on a table (minus the fifty-six Minor Arcana cards) and the "forty gods" contained within the tarot images are then invoked.

These three varieties of the tarot—the tarocchi, tarochinni and Minchiate—represent the three primary types available on the market today. Of course, there are many other national and regional varieties such as those of Switzerland using bells, shields, roses and acorns as suit emblems instead of the customary cups, coins, rods and swords. Most tarot-derived playing cards currently in use also tend to have dropped the all-important trumps, even those maintaining the original suit emblems, such as the deck used in Spain and South America for the game of Rocambor.

Characteristic with the spirit of the Renaissance, the quaint medievalized mnemonic images of the fifteenth-century tarot were already being reinvested once more with their old pagan forms. The set supposedly created by the artist Andrea Mantegna, but more probably by Baccio Baldini, in 1470 or 1485, returns to the old pagan images, heavily classicized. Interestingly, in this particular instance they appear to have reverted to their original use as a memory system as opposed to merely a deck of playing cards. They are made of flimsy paper and are much too large to play with. The artist who made them used only fifty images, five sets of ten. Differing opinions have been put forward as to who originally commissioned them and for what purpose. One theory maintains they were evolved as a quasi-theological memory game on the familiar lines by the cardinals Johannes Bessarion, Nicholas of Cusa and Pope Pius II to relieve the tedium of a seven-month-long ecclesiastical council held at Mantua in 1459.*

The first rank depicts the conditions of man, ranging from beggar to supreme pontiff; the second the nine classical muses led by the Greco-Roman god of art, Apollo; the third, the ten liberal arts and sciences; the fourth, the three cosmic principles of astronomy, chronology and geography followed by the seven virtues; the fifth and last, the seven planets of astrology and the spheres of the zodiac, primum mobile and first cause, or absolute. From beggar to God in ten relatively easy steps comprehensible to the educated Renaissance mind. It is said that the German painter and engraver Albrecht Dürer saw these tarot images when he visited Italy in 1494 and, inspired by them, produced his own Gothically styled set.

By mid-Renaissance pagan gods and heroes had been widely accepted as artistic metaphors. On a considerably lower level, the characters of the Italian *commedia dell'arte* also exhibited characteristics imputed by medieval scholars to the ancient gods. Arlecchino appears to have distinctly mercurial traits, complete with multicolored garment, magic baton and invisibility, even on occasions impersonating Mercury. Colombine, "the

---

*H. Brockhaus, "Ein Geduldspiel, die Leitung der Welt oder die Himmelsleiter, die Sogenannten Taroks Mantegnas vom Jahre 1459-60," in *Miscellanea di storia dell'arte in onore di I. B. Supino* (Florence, 1933).

dove," shows the amatory inclinations of that bird's mistress, Lady Venus. The miserly Venetian, ancient slippered Pantaloon, has much in him of Saturn, while the boastful Scaramouche, Skirmish or Captain Fracasse, has an obviously martial air about him. The gullible and hedonistic Dr. Gratiano appears as either lawyer, doctor or priest, all three guises of the medieval Jupiter. Pulcinello, the Apulian rascal who in later times becomes the malicious puppet character Punch, shows a striking similarity in his antics to Hercules.

The popular iconography of the time was all-pervasive. It filtered into literature and fed back again into the common stock of legend and story. By the time of the late Renaissance, the Elizabethan and Jacobean dramatists of England and France had used and reused the old pagan themes and characters time and again, changed, distorted, reinvested with contemporary values, but still containing at their core the same old pagan archetypes.

By the seventeenth century many of the older varieties of tarot packs had disappeared, to be replaced by the simpler decks we know today containing the familiar suit signs—hearts, spades, diamonds and clubs.

It is not until the eighteenth century that we can again pick up the thread of documented tarot history. Though traditions of memory magic had been maintained within those last sanctuaries of Gnosticism, the Masonic and Rosicrucian lodges, the lowly tarot had only managed to preserve its existence as at best a pack of gypsy fortune-telling cards, at worst a game.

And this is where our Egyptian theory was evolved. In 1781, eight years before the French Revolution, the theory that the gypsy tarot was the remains of an ancient Egyptian book of magical wisdom, treasured by the Romany peoples since their exodus from their native land of Egypt, was proposed by Antoine Court de Gébelin, a French occultist and archeologist. He published it in a nine-volume book called *Le Monde Primitif analysé et comparé avec le monde moderne* (*The Primitive World analysed and compared to the modern world*). Gébelin was a Freemason, much preoccupied with the mysteries of the ancients, especially with the secret lore imputed to the ancient Egyptians, as was then fashionable.

As the clue to deciphering Egyptian hieroglyphics had not yet been provided by the Rosetta stone, many portentous secrets were said to lie in the writings of the Egyptians. This was not a new theory, however. From the time of the Islamic empire, roughly A.D. 900-1100, Egypt had been singled out in many wizards' minds as the place where the most potent magical secrets had originated. The word "alchemy" itself derives from the Arabic, meaning the art of Khem, or Egypt. And the occultists of the eighteenth century were right in their assumptions, as we shall see—but only up to a certain point. Most Western magical symbolism, including that of the tarot images, had indeed emanated from the Near East, but the Near East of the post-Christian era, of Alexandria and Byzantium, as opposed to that of the ancient pharaohs. De Gébelin and his fellow Rosicrucians were right in place but wrong in time. Succeeding Rosicrucian generations have speculated further and added accumulations of lore to the mysterious deck. The rumored original was claimed to be none other than the ancient and mythical *Book of Thoth*, written by the hand of the god Thoth himself when he descended from the high heavens and first walked the earth among men.

Within this book were said to be two potent and all-embracing formulas. By reading the first, the operator would be able to cast an enchantment upon the sky, the earth, the world of the night, the mountains and the waters of the deep; he would, like Solomon, understand the language of the birds and reptiles, and by means of the spell's magical power he could hover over the water and perceive all the fish as far down as the deepest abyss in the sea. The second formula, no less puissant than the first, gave victory over the tomb, earthly immortality, and a vision of the Sun and Moon in their divine forms surrounded by their retinue of gods.

This formula contains all the important elements of the latter-day cult of Isis that Lucius Apuleius, the Roman author, was initiated into and wrote guardedly about in his work of fiction, *The Golden Ass*:

> ... I approached the limits of the dead; I trod upon the threshold of Proserpina [the goddess of death] and I was carried beyond the spheres of the elements. I saw the sun shining brilliantly at midnight, and approached the Gods of the Underworld, and those from On High; and I worshipped them face to face. ...

Again this identification of the tarot seems to contain an element of truth. The trump cards undoubtedly derive in part from some such cult, and it was in this mystical sense that the tarot was adopted and popularized by eighteenth-century occultists. Wolfgang Mozart, an ardent Freemason, made use of a similar Egyptian initiatory story in the libretto of *The Magic Flute*.

However, when referring to the *Book of Thoth*, it would serve our purposes better if we were to refer to the god Thoth by his Greek name, Hermes Trismegistos, meaning "Thrice Great Hermes." The name itself is very revealing. The Romans called him Mercury, and in postclassical times he was held to be the god of magic and metallurgy whom one must invoke before attempting any alchemical operation. Many of the Gnostically inspired works devoted to alchemy and astrology claimed authorship from him as "Thrice Great Hermes," in much the same way that many of the magical conjuring books and memory manuals were imputed to the penmanship of the prolific King Solomon.

Though alchemy and astrology lay at the respectable end of the occult spectrum, actual attempts to direct the stars and forces dealt with by these two sciences often edged uncomfortably into the area of sorcery, which lay at the other end. So did the tarot. Bernardino certainly had no doubts about that. Prior to its eighteenth-century rehabilitation by de Gébelin, the deck was to all intents and purposes quite unknown in Paris, used only by diviners in outlying districts, the gypsies of southern France and Italian *strege* and *streghoni*.

With the appearance of de Gébelin's book, almost overnight the tarot became the tool of Rosicrucian sages par excellence, feted as the bible of all true occultists. It took only the ingenuity of a nineteenth-century apostate priest, the French Rosicrucian writer and cabalist Eliphas Lévi, whose books were the major inspiration of the nineteenth-century occult revival, to discover an apparent link between the twenty-two letters of the Hebrew alphabet and the cards of the Major Arcana.

To the cabalist, each of the twenty-two Hebrew letters signifies a special spiritual power. Hence an alliance between these letters and the twenty-two trumps gives an immediate cabalistic interpretation to them.

Most of the books written about tarot cards have pursued Lévi's line of thought. Unfortunately, far from elucidating the cards, this often seems to add confusion to an already mysterious subject. The mind boggles at some of the metaphysical straitjackets which have been strapped upon the cards over the years.

The deck is generally stretched upon a cabalistic Procrustean bed and what fails to be accommodated is either ignored or shrugged off as a "blind to the uninitiated." And this for the most part is how tarot is interpreted today. Though the memory-magic that lay behind the use of tarot cards was preserved within Rosicrucian lodges, it wore an ill-fitting Judeo-Christian mask. Only in so far as Christian and Judaic supernatural lore can be said to be imbued with pagan beliefs and doctrines can the tarot be said to reflect either of these two traditions, as we shall see in the following chapter.

CHAPTER 3

𝕿𝖆𝖗𝖔𝖙 𝕾𝖔𝖗𝖈𝖊𝖗𝖞

We have surveyed the little there is of documented tarot history. Now let us examine the occult uses the tarots were put to and where these practices have led to. To do this we must understand a little about the occult theories which lay behind them.

Nowadays people are finding it less and less hard to believe in things like ESP or "second sight," especially in view of the intangibilities presented by modern science. After all, who has seen an electron with his naked eye? Yet we know such things exist.

Today we have a young, quite legitimate science called parapsychology growing up, which attempts to build rational constructs to explain seemingly irrational extrasensory perception and its less widely recognized sister phenomenon psychokinesis, or mind over matter.

As the roots of such psychic powers were once considered to lie in the realm of the soul, an uncertain and speculative field preempted by theology, the range of such faculties was optimistically considered to be practically unlimited, disobeying all known laws of time and space. When occultism came to be organized in a more scientific form during the nineteenth century, the old idea of the omnipotence of psychic power remained entrenched. If anybody suspected that ESP, for instance, might be hindered in some way by physical barriers such as distance, nobody had any way of proving it. Bona fide, repeatable instances of ESP one hundred percent acceptable to the impartial observer are hard to come by in any event. Hence, to the eighteenth- and nineteenth-century scientist an experiment to see if ESP behaved similarly to electromagnetic radiation or sound waves—whether or not the time lapse could be measured between the point of emission of the signal and the point of reception; whether the distance between target and percipient affected the outcome in any way—was really doomed to failure on account of the unsophisticated measuring apparatus at his disposal. It is only recently, through the advances of technology and the use of the complex mathematics of statistics, that today's scientists of the occult, the parapsychologists, are beginning to discover that ESP and related powers are not so unlimited in scope; that they do seem to obey natural laws of their own, which may one day be fitted quite gracefully into a universal scheme alongside the inverse square law and all the other axioms of physical science.* ESP may, in fact, turn out to be a method of biological energy transmission by means of such elusive subatomic carrier particles as neutrinos. Levitation and psychokinesis may finally be found to be caused by the subject's extrusion of "nervous" energy, now suspected but as yet unproven. Each day brings new and more refined technical equipment into existence which is at last rendering easier the parapsychologist's task of tracking down and identifying the mysterious and fleeting ESP powers.

So from that point of view the more esoteric aspects of sorcery look as though they are destined to become part of science one day, even as hypnotism, Greek fire, pharmaceutical drugs and the alchemical knowledge of metals have done in the past. But the wholehearted acceptance of psi by the entire scientific world still seems a long way off.

*See Karlis Osis and Malcolm E. Turner, Jr., "Distance and ESP: A Transcontinental Experiment," *Proceedings of the American Society of Psychical Research*, Vol. 27 (September, 1968).

Any attempt, ancient or modern, to rationalize the psi powers has always required some basic theory to show how the universe hangs together, how all the parts interrelate. And most of these theories are similar if not identical. The old doctrine of archetypes was one such theory. It lay behind medieval astrology and all the occult sciences, such as alchemy, chiromancy and numerology. It has been with us in one form or another as far back as we can remember, achieving its height in the mysticism of India and such philosophies as those of Pythagoras, Plato and Henri Louis Bergson. Basically, it consists of the notion that all existing things, including people, are the end products—projections, reflections, if you will—of some greater, ultimate reality, which one might designate as "spiritual," although nobody is sure quite what that term means. The everyday world we experience is the realm of reflections and illusion. We have a foothold in the world of the real, inasmuch as we exist "down here" and, therefore, axiomatically "up there" also. The old magical dictum *quod superius, sicut inferius* ("as above, so below"), refers to this basic underlying wizard's belief.

Between this world and that there exists, moreover, a sort of halfway house. This in-between world is the medium of communication between the real and the reflection. You may think of it metaphorically as a lens or mirror which focuses the light rays streaming from the real to produce the reflection. But here the metaphor breaks down, for this mirror, or astral world as it is called by many modern occultists, is far from an inert and passive recipient of light. On the contrary, it is a two-way system, a true channel of communication between the here-and-now world and that of the real. We can, if we know how, make changes in our world of here-and-now by intercepting and altering the impulses we receive from the world of the real while they are still "filtering through" this halfway house and before they get a chance to "crystallize out" down here. (I use quotation marks advisedly because we are speaking very much in the area of analogy.)

In occult terminology, the "lower" levels of this astral plane impinge upon the everyday world, just as the "higher" connect with the supernal world. In fact, the world of here-and-now may be said to actually grow out of the lower astral, which in turn grows out of the higher levels. Theosophical occultists, who have organized this traditional lore into a system of arcane physics largely inspired by Indian philosophy, refer to the lowest astral level as the etheric, making a subplane out of it.

It is helpful to think of these otherworlds in terms more of radio wavelengths than of actual places. When you progress "up" the astral plane, you are in effect tuning your radio receiver to a higher wavelength. At first your regular signals will become overlaid with those from the next wave band (as happens involuntarily in a psychotic breakdown), and then as you move yet higher, these signals themselves will take precedence and the lower ones vanish completely. These signals are what an occultist is alluding to when he speaks about "vibrations." The vibrations of an object or place are the astral forces that radiate from it. Its psychic framework, if you like. A person who believes in the possibility of intervening upon these higher planes or wave bands to produce material effects "down here" is a fairly accurate definition of the word "occultist"—someone who seeks to study the hidden laws behind nature, thus in some measure anticipating and controlling coming events in a way which might appear miraculous to an outsider ignorant of the subtle forces that are being brought into play.

A naturally born occultist—a person born with an unlearned and often unconscious ability to perform this spiritual engineering—is what we today refer to as a "psychic," "medium" or "sensitive." Often his ability will manifest in a specific manner so that parapsychologists will refer to him as a "clairvoyant," a "telepath" or a "psychokineticist" (levitator). Now primitive man has always found it easier to characterize these subtle forces of the psyche as gods, demons or spirits—the terminology changes from religion to religion. As his thought processes become more sophisticated, there is greater demand for rationalization of these beliefs. Many early religions were thus intellectualized into philosophies, subtler and more complicated than the dark cults from which they originally sprang, although very often their supernatural elements were retained. What previously had been a hierarchy of gods now became a system of forces.

This is, in fact, what took place between the second and fourth centuries A.D. among many of the Mediterranean pagan cults which had resisted the rise of monastic Christianity. They joined forces—for example, one aspect of the Asian worship of Cybele being seen to complement another of maybe the Egyptian Isis cult. In this manner a "theosophy" or divine wisdom came into existence, a grand universal religion, tor which the philosophical basis had been laid down partly centuries before by the Greek philosophers Pythagoras and Plato. In fact, the adherents of this syncretic paganism are often referred to as Neoplatonists.

During the Renaissance, along with the general reevaluation of the pagan past which was taking place all over Europe, Neoplatonic ideas again became current, even fashionable, in scholarly circles. Because it was a system founded upon Greek philosophy it was more or less tolerated by the papacy. However, if study of it led to any form of *practical* application, the situation could come perilously close to heresy.

Italian philosophers like Pico della Mirandola and Marsilio Ficino evolved a theory about this relationship of the world of mortals to the spiritual on Neoplatonic lines. They considered the universe to be a vast, universal machine, with all the parts miraculously interacting, a living entity in its own right, a sort of slumbering cosmic giant which was known as the *anima mundi* or world soul. You and I and, indeed, everything in existence were merely thoughts drifting through this vast entity's mind, "such stuff as dreams are made on."

The Renaissance Neoplatonists considered that within the *anima mundi* certain independent dream entities existed rather like parasites on a host animal or dissociated complexes swimming around in the depths of the psyche. These great beings, larger and more powerful than mere mortals, did not always cast reflections like you or me in the world of here-and-now, although many of them did. They were known variously as powers and principalities, archons, angels or simply gods, depending on what philosophical beliefs were held. They were the larger, original versions of many smaller earthly copies, hence another of their titles, "archetypes." We were the small cogs in the machinery of the *anima mundi*; they were the big wheels. It was the activity of these archetypes that was said to lie behind the laws of nature, including such apparently preordained matters as the courses of the stars and planets. In the case of the latter, the archetype was known as the planetary spirit of Mars or Venus—the sphere's guiding intelligence. It was through the use of the names and images of ancient gods, who were the originals of these archetypes, that the medieval magician sought to contact such beings. These names were thought to possess the power of calling the archetypes into activity; they were analogous to magical telephone numbers to the archetypal world, the perforated programming cards of a computer, or the keys to a lock. By using these notae to attune deep levels of his mind to the archetypes, by imprinting their special symbols strongly on his imagination and thereby entering into a close mental rapport with them, the wizard aimed to transform his own psyche into a small edition of the *anima mundi*. How close and yet how far the church was from the truth in its belief in the sorcerer's intimacy with demons and the resulting loss of soul. This union with the *anima mundi* accomplished, nature would obey the adept's whim as surely as the planets follow their ordained courses. She could not do other wise, for the wizard's purposes had become united with those of the world soul. The powers resulting from the great union were said to be almost limitless. The transformation of the elements, that ancient alchemical goal, became feasible. Fire and flood lay at the adept's beck and call. The weather was his to command. Within the field of human affairs, the warlock's power was equally impressive, manifesting itself in what today we would consider a remarkable hypnotic ability, known then as "fascination," "enchantment" or simply the art of "binding." By exercising this power, the sorcerer deluded the senses of his subjects, producing apparent changes of shape in himself or others, including invisibility, and the induction of profound sleep among onlookers.

Stories concerning the legendary wielders of such powers abound in bardic legend and medieval literature—Celtic druids such as Broichan and Diancecht; Dark Age enchanters as Merlin and Vergilius and sorceresses Hellawes and Morgan le Fay; medieval wizards Faustus, Vandermast, Roger Bacon and Michael Scot—all woven into the fabric of romance now, but in ages past rather something more, for most of them were once real people.

In medieval and Renaissance Europe a practicing occultist could be known by a variety of names: witch, warlock, wizard, sorcerer or magus, among others—although most of these titles have particular specialized meanings. Generally speaking, the first three may be said to apply to occultists whose beliefs are drawn from vestigial pagan beliefs, often bound up in the form of a religious cult. The titles "sorcerer" or "magus," on the other hand, have come to refer to those who remain within the Judeo-Christian fold and think of occult powers in terms of opposing forces of good and evil, angels and fiends. Both witch and magus systems, however, derive from a common source, and the distinction between them was very academic, as sharper members of the Holy Inquisition were quick to realize. Generally speaking, medieval and Renaissance scholars who wished to study the occult arts for whatever reasons found it safer to introduce a distinction between "white" and "black" magic, which did not necessarily mean "good" or "evil" magic but rather "permitted Christian" as opposed to "forbidden pagan." This plea for distinction was not always successful. It was a fine line to tread, and such unlucky practitioners as the sixteenth-century sorcerer-monk Giordano Bruno overstepped it and were roasted alive despite all their protestations of "magia not goetia!" "Magia" simply means white magic; "goetia," black.

In theory, magia was a permissible species of magic, conducted through the services of angels as opposed to those of demons, which was goetia. It is from "magia" that our words "magic" and "magician" derive; the word itself comes from the Latin word *magus*, which originally referred to a priest of the ancient Persian fire-cult of Ahura-Mazda. You will recall that the three wise men who came to worship at the crib of the infant Jesus are sometimes spoken of as "Magi." Magian beliefs were seen by Christian apologists for magic, such as Heinrich Cornelius Agrippa von Nettesheim, as a holy, God-given science of miracles which was practiced millennia ago by the holy men of the East, including certain wise rabbis of Israel, who subsequently formulated it into the cabala.

Goetia, on the other hand—stemming from the Greek word *goes*, meaning witchcraft—meant pagan and therefore satanic magic. A person who practiced it was simply a witch or a wizard.

The unscholarly practitioner, of course, made no such distinction, and should he be caught at his art, he had to settle for the by then despised title of witch or wizard, whether he liked it or not. There would be no possibility of a learned defense using the subtle distinctions between magian or goetic operations.

Goetia at its blackest was, from the point of view of the Roman Church, the deliberate invocation of devils, resulting in a wicked personal relationship being set up between the wizard and members of the infernal hierarchy; it usually included the loss of the conjurer's soul into the bargain. The legend of Faust illustrates well what the church imagined was the usual course of events. Any hidden devotion to old pagan gods would, of course, be viewed in this light.

Most medieval *grimoires* maintained a sitting-on-the-fence approach, taking the best of both pagan and Christian worlds and·conjuring the pagan devils by Hebrew and, later, Christian divine names and theological terms. Many of these old pagan deities remain to be seen in their grotesque devils' disguises, even if the *grimoire* writer had no idea who they were.

In the infernal hierarchy of the *Lesser Key of Solomon*, for instance, Horus, the hawk-headed sun god of ancient Egypt, has become the fiery Haures or Flauros. Ashtoreth, the moon goddess, a Mesopotamian version of Isis, changes sex and becomes Astarot of the Stinking Breath, a mighty duke riding upon a dragon. The Persian deity Aeshma Daeva becomes Asmodeus. The Syrian storm god Baal turns into the Oriental demon-king Bael who, according to the Lemegeton, ". . . appeareth in divers shapes, sometimes like a Cat, sometimes like a toad, and sometimes like a man, and sometimes all these forms at once. . . ." (See Figure 19.)

Figure 19

It is quite apparent that these goetic demon images are drawn from the same source as the symbols of the *ars notaria*-type memory manuals and astrology, namely paganism via Gnosticism.

One of the widely acknowledged masters of magic of the sixteenth century, Heinrich Cornelius Agrippa von Nettesheim, indicates that he is aware of these sources for the goetia when, in the customary disclaimer to black magic that every prudent magician of the time included in his written works, he refers to the vast gulf existing between his magic and that of certain wicked "gnostic and Templar magicians. . . . "* Far be it that his lore should stem from such an infernal stock!

Writing in the fourteenth century, the Moorish philosopher, jurist, historian and scholar ibn-Khaldun expounds the theory that the sorcerer derives his power by planting certain images and pictures within his imagination, images of the stars, planets and "devils."†

The thirteenth-century alchemist Albertus Magnus likewise writes how he had come across a prescription for this power of sorcery within a work of the philosopher Avicenna and had proved to himself by experiment that when the emotions are stimulated strongly and combined with the use of appropriate harmonious astrological or magical notae, events can be altered in conformation with the individual's will, without apparent physical intervention.**

Many stories exist bearing testimony to Albertus' legendary prowess in this form of wizardry. One of them tells how on one occasion Albertus invited certain guests to dine at his house in Cologne, among whom was Count William of Holland. The guests were somewhat annoyed to find that Albertus had arranged for the meal to be eaten outdoors, even though it was the middle of winter and snow was thick on the ground. The wizard insisted, much to everyone's irritation, and told them that their worries were groundless and all would be well. This was cold comfort, but the guests obediently took their seats and the meal began. Hardly had the first mouthful been taken when the mischievous sorcerer made a gesture, and with it the entire wintery landscape vanished from before the eyes of his astonished friends to be replaced by one indicative of high summer—trees in leaf, flowers blossoming and birds singing!

These two instances are our first practical hints of the forbidden uses that the memory notae were put to.

---

*Heinrich Cornelius Agrippa von Nettesheim, *De Occulta Philosophia* (Antwerp, 1531), pp. 54-55.

†ibn-Khaldun, *Muqaddimah*, trans. by F. Rosenthal (London, Routledge & Kegan Paul, 1967).

**Albertus Magnus, *De Mirabilibus Mundi* (Cologne, 1485).

In fact, the symbols themselves were to become the magical building blocks for most medieval and Renaissance talismans.

A talisman was simply a "charged" nota, a sort of psychic battery that you could carry around with you, usually designed to achieve a certain aim, such as "the favor of princes" or "protection on journeys by water."

The wizard-monk Joannes Trithemius provides us with an early instance of the use of one of these images. This mysterious abbot who lived in the fifteenth and early sixteenth centuries is thought by many to have been the European grand master of a secret college of magical lore, possibly the Rosicrucians. He certainly appears to have been the nucleus around which a small group of known warlocks gathered. Heinrich Cornelius Agrippa and Philippus Aureolus Paracelsus, that other great master of magic, were personal students of his, as were the demonologists Johann Wier and Jacques Gohory, albeit second-generation ones through Agrippa. The Elizabethan astrologer and magician Dr. John Dee knew and valued his writings highly. Those works of Trithemius that attracted most attention were two small manuscripts which were prudently not published in book form until 1606, ninety years after the abbot's death. The work was entitled *Steganographia*, and it dealt with cabalistic methods of encoding messages in symbols and then communicating the resultant symbols by means of a power that today we would call telepathy. The method used was a planetary nota process. In this instance a permitted "angelicized" figure of the power of Saturn called Orifiel was to be drawn in a specified manner and activated with a suitably holy formula. The message would be transmitted to the desired person without any intermediary via the *anima mundi*, wherever he was in the world, usually within the period of a day.

Agrippa made use of this occult telephone by his own admission,* and no doubt John Dee may have found it invaluable in his espionage activities conducted abroad for England's Queen Elizabeth I. Some occultists believe that many of the magical

---

*Heinrich Cornelius Agrippa von Nettesheim, *De Occulta Philosophia* (Antwerp, 1531).

séances conducted by Dee were in fact nothing other than "sending and receiving" sessions of such clandestine information. The methods he adopted could easily lend themselves to such ends. The recipient seated himself before a crystal and after suitable preparations entered a trance and perceived an "angelic" figure within the globe. This figure almost invariably held a rod within its hand, and by means of this indicated certain letters arranged acrosticwise within a square table beside it. The seer would call out the reference point of the square indicated, such as "two along, five down," and his assistant, usually Dr. Dee himself, would find the relevant square containing a letter in a similar table he had at hand. A variety of tables were used for this, and the specific one to be worked with was indicated at the beginning of the seance. Each table had a name, such as the table of fire, or the table of air, and the area within each was also divided up into smaller ones likewise referred to by elemental names. So when the seer described the figure as pointing to "the fourth square along, three down, of the air angle of fire," Dr. Dee would know immediately which square and therefore which letter the spirit was indicating. By a combination of this spelling process and Trithemius' image magic, very specific messages theoretically could be sent.*

The material that Dee obtained through his crystal-gazing experiments was later incorporated into the teachings of the last of the great magical societies that followed in the scholarly tradition of Albertus Magnus and Agrippa: the Hermetic Order of the Golden Dawn. It claimed to be the inheritor of the ancient keys to psychic power handed down from one generation of adepts to another. We have already come across its trail in Chapter 1.

It was founded in the latter half of the nineteenth century by three erudite English Rosicrucians—Wynn Westcott, S. L. Macgregor Mathers and Dr. William K. Woodman—and it was from its teachings that much, if not most, twentieth-century European ritual occultism derives.

The Golden Dawn's teachings and rituals essentially consisted

*See Meric Casaubon, *A True and Faithful Relation of What Passed for Many Years Between Dr. John Dee and Some Spirits* (London, 1659).

of a blend of theosophy, the magical cabalism of Eliphas Lévi, and Egyptian Rosicrucian ceremonies typical of the seventeenth and eighteenth centuries. Throughout the course of its existence, including that of its various offshoot groups, it has included among its members such personalities as the writer A. E. Waite; the Irish poet William Butler Yeats; Algernon Blackwood; actress Florence Farr; Annie Horniman, the benefactor of the Horniman Museum; Bram Stoker, the author of *Dracula*; the supposed Satanist Aleister Crowley; cabalists Dion Fortune, Israel Regardie and Paul Foster Case; and the writers Evelyn Underhill and Charles Williams. It is rumored that at one point Sax Rohmer, the author of the Fu Manchu books, also belonged.

The central purpose of the society was basically the achievement of mystical illumination and magical power. It aimed at turning its members into magi, albeit with the worthy Rosicrucian proviso that the aspirant "desire to know in order that he might serve." The chief symbol that the group used in its teachings was the cabalistic glyph known as the Tree of Life (see Figure 20).

This complex symbol is basically a mystical ground plan of the way the universe came into existence. Based upon the medieval philosophy of Spanish Judaism known as the cabala, it proposed a system of "emanations" responsible for the creation of the cosmos. The theory, which comprised a blend of religion and metaphysics, argued that God, the "unmanifest," wishing to create the universe, "overflowed" into manifestation, creating the first sphere or wavelength of existence, which was known as "Kether," "the Crown." When this wavelength was complete, the divine power again overflowed, creating the next wavelength down the scale, "Wisdom" or "Chokmah;" and so on down to the tenth level, which is called "Malkuth," "the Kingdom," and refers to our here-and-now world.

As you see, this is a medieval variety of the astral plane theory we have just been looking at. Each of the spheres on the Tree of Life corresponds to one of the wavelengths or bands of vibration upon the astral plane, *anima mundi*, or whatever else

Figure 20

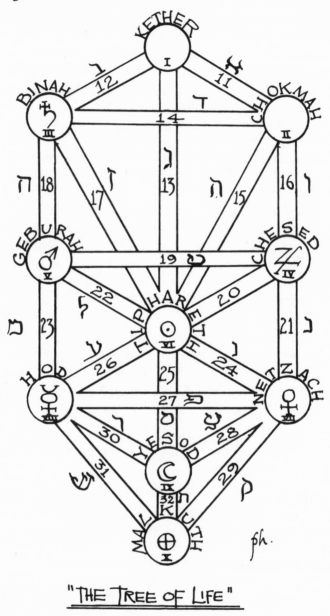

"THE TREE OF LIFE"

you wish to call it. This "doctrine of emanations" which is contained in the Tree of Life arrangement did not, however, originate with Judaism but came from those fountains of modern European magical lore, Gnosticism and Neoplatonism.

According to the pre-Copernican Ptolemaic astronomical theory closely allied with this doctrine of emanations, the seven astrological planets in descending order (Saturn, Jupiter, Mars, Sun, Venus, Mercury, Moon) were created with each successive outpouring of power. Each planet symbolized, and was therefore said to "govern," some particular aspect of human behavior, such as Mars, wrath and courage; Venus, love; and Mercury, cunning. This, of course, is the basis of all present-day astrological readings. The planets themselves were associated with the pagan deities whose names they bore, and in cabalistic speculation they all hung like celestial fruit upon the tree of life.

Now this symbol of a tree with its roots in the underworld and its branches embracing the stars is one of the easiest pictures of the cosmos a person can form in his mind. Because of this it is also one of the most ancient, occurring throughout the world in all times and places. To the Nordic wizard it was the tree Yggdrasil; to the medieval cabalist, the Tree of Life. The Babylonians symbolized it by the ziggurat, pyramid of seven planetary levels; and the Gnostics thought of it as the heavenly "klimax," or ladder. Siberian shamans likewise see it as a magical tree or ladder, and the Indian yogi as a pillar of unfolding lotuses set within his own body. On it stand the images of the primordial gods, each reigning within his own mansion or sphere. The mental climbing of such a spiritual ladder to awaken the powers of each level by means of their magical notae was the forbidden secret of the medieval memory systems, and men like Giordano Bruno perished for openly teaching such doctrines. The Golden Dawn taught a similar doctrine in cabalistic terms.

As we saw earlier, the apostate priest Eliphas Lévi had assigned each of the twenty-two tarot trumps to one of the twenty-two "paths" upon the Tree of Life. He had also followed traditions laid down by Pietro d'Abano and Agrippa in the Middle Ages and later consolidated by the nineteenth-century wizard Francis Barratt,* in allocating each of the four letters of the Tetragrammaton to one of the Aristotelian elements, the so-called "elements of the wise." Thus:

>J   (Yod)—fire
>H   (Heh)—water
>V   (Vau)—air
>H   (Heh final)—earth)

The Tetragrammaton was theoretically the supreme magical word of power, the cabalists' name of God, the correct pronunciation of which, thought to be known only to adepts and high priests in direct line of succession to Aaron and Moses, could cause the universe to bend to the will of the user. In the Bible it is rendered "Jehovah," but the Hebrew spelling only indicates the consonants J H V H. The secret of the correct pronunciation of such names was thought to be the most guarded secret of the cabalistic schools of the Middle Ages.† Lévi claimed furthermore that each of the four elements was represented by one of the tarot Minor Arcana emblems, thus giving the following scheme:

>J   fire—rod
>H   water—cup
>V   air—sword
>H   earth—coin

Each of the spheres of the Tree of Life was said to have four distinct levels of function—the mundane, which was responsible for the planetary sphere; the angelic, lower astral; the archangelic, higher astral; and finally, the divine or archetypal—thus producing "forty worlds" of manifestation. These four levels are said by cabalists to be none other than the four component letters of the mysterious Tetragrammaton.

Each path or sphere of this tree could be used to file symbolically associated images under their relevant tarot card heading—the old memory-file technique again.

*Francis Barratt, *The Magus* (New York, University Books, 1967).

†See G. G. Scholem, *Major Trends in Jewish Mysticism* (New York, Schocken Books, 1961).

For instance, the spiritual archetype or force which reveals itself in the symbol of the Sun in its glory was also said traditionally to manifest itself under the images of a lion, a child or a phoenix. The metal gold also came under this solar heading. So did frankincense, wine, and the acacia, bay, laurel and vine leaves. In medieval days this scheme of archetypal pigeonholing came to be known as the Doctrine of Signatures, a term coined by Paracelsus. Pharmaceutically it was nonsense, of course, but poetically and psychologically it made a certain sense. By associating colors, odors, sounds, numbers and images in an associative chain, when you pick up the thread of one, say the color gold, the rest will unfold within your mind quite naturally: gold—sun—phoenix—flames—pyramid—frankincense—child, and so on. In effect, by practicing this type of discipline you can turn your imagination loose *within a controlled area* of your mind like a rabbit within a pen.

Now whether there is any validity to the theory that these chains of association constitute a reality that is "already there" in some way or they are purely artificial and conditioned is a matter of great controversy among occultists. Certainly W. B. Yeats and the literary French Symbolist movement, heavily influenced by Lévi, considered the former to be the case; that numbers, words, sounds, colors, scents and things in general were all subtly and inextricably linked together in certain pre-ordained webs and chains via the *anima mundi*. It is a poetic concept. But the phenomenon on which it is based is a real one.

Synesthesia is the scientific name for it. Francis Galton, an early nineteenth-century researcher in the field, wrote that one of his subjects experienced the alphabetical letter "A" as "pure white, and like china in texture. 'E,' red, not transparent; vermilion with china white would represent it. 'I,' light, bright yellow. . . ."[*] Similarly, many composers, such as Walter Wolfgang Goethe[†] or Aleksandr N. Scriabin have associated notes of

---

[*]Francis Galton, *Inquiries into Human Faculty* (London, Macmillan & Co., Ltd., 1883).

[†]See *Goethe's Theory of Colours*, trans. by Charles Eastlake (London, John Murray, 1840). Also see the diaries of Paul Klee and Vasili Kandinski. Also A. R. Luria, *The Mind of a Mnemonist*, trans. by Lynn Solotaroff (New York, Discus Books, 1969).

the musical scale with certain colors, as painters such as Vasili Kandinski and Paul Klee have also done. But no one is consistent. The ways in which the colors, scents or sounds are linked are more likely to be peculiar to the individual. One person might see green as soothing, another as sinister. This might be considered the Pavlov school of interpretation: the bell rings and the dog's mouth waters solely because he has been conditioned. We associate "green" with "envy" solely because we have been taught to do so. Most occultists fall somewhere in between two extremes, maintaining that the majority of our associations are indeed learned, though underlying all is the a priori substratum of astral archetypes, by means of which we interpret everyday reality around us. They are as "built in" as the crystal lattice in the saline solution before crystallization occurs.

Thus, in the estimation of Lévi and the Golden Dawn, by linking the twenty-two trump cards with the paths of the tree the tarot appeared to provide a grand hieroglyph through which the magus could work his will on the universe.

Essentially it supplied the key to the astral planes. By using it to project his consciousness onto these planes, the Golden Dawn adept hoped to impose his will upon the symbolic astral "flora and fauna" he encountered and thus alter reality before it filtered down into the here-and-now world, crystallized on the mundane level.

Now there are various hit-and-miss methods used by occultists to gain access to these "higher planes" in trance. Often drugs such as datura and hashish are used to open the door. The two most widely used nondrug methods besides the "body of light" technique of the Golden Dawn were stumbled upon by non-Rosicrucians.

Sylvan Muldoon was born in 1902 and spend most of his life in the Midwest of the United States. He grew up among spiritualists, where ideas of "astral projection" were not uncommon. Muldoon, who spent much of his time in bed due to frequent periods of ill-health, began to discover that he appeared to have the involuntary power of "slipping out of his body," like a hand out of a glove, and while in this state of disembodiment wandering about at will in what appeared to be a nebulous "astral" copy of his physical body.

Having a lot of time on his hands, Muldoon began to experiment with these hallucinations and soon found that there appeared to be very definite laws governing the release of this "astral double." He also found that the scenes he witnessed at different remote locations while in his apparently extruded condition often seemed to have actually taken place in the way he experienced them.

It is not an unknown phenomenon in the annals of occultism. Early psychical researchers, the prototypes of our present-day parapsychologists, would have labeled it "traveling clairvoyance." In the lore of witchcraft, it was known as "sending the fetch."

Muldoon found that at first he was not always able to effect an astral projection at will. He had to evolve a method of "tricking" himself into projecting. In fact, all he was learning was that the deeper areas of our unconscious mind, where these powers lie dormant, are not accessible to frontal attack. The language of the deep mind is not rational logic but rather emotional need. Most of Muldoon's out-of-the-body excursions were undertaken while he was asleep in bed. In the middle of a dream he would "awaken" to find himself apparently held in the grip of some invisible force and hovering horizontally above his bed. He would initially be unable to move his limbs but with an effort of will soon found he was capable of locomotion. It was with a shock that he soon discovered he was suspended above the bed upon which his own physical body still lay in deep sleep!

The method by which Muldoon tricked his deep mind into cooperating was a simple one. According to theory, the astral body is an exact subtle duplicate of the physical and spends most of its time enmeshed with it. Assuming this, it seemed to Muldoon that the astral might exhibit the same reaction patterns and physical needs as its material counterpart did, out of alignment as well as in. Therefore, in order to dislodge his astral body, Muldoon arranged to experience a physical need such as thirst or hunger in the night, having previously made sure that his material body was in some way hampered from answering it. Occultists occasionally accomplish this by suspending themselves in a slinglike device known as a "witches' cradle" which induces all the required symptoms of sensory deprivation.* However, Muldoon did not need to resort to such methods. He had observed that on returning to his physical body after an astral excursion, its limbs would be caught in the same cataleptic grip as he had experienced in his astral body at the beginning of the projection. He reasoned that his astral body had only moved out of coincidence with its rigid material counterpart because it was the only part of him capable at the time of moving to answer the frantic messages flashed by his deep mind. Muldoon linked this cataleptic state of "incapacity" with the chronic attacks of ill-health he suffered throughout his life. So the answer for him was to try to induce this state of incapacity—a rather dangerous practice in his condition, one would have thought—by such methods as previous fasting, "willing" his pulse rate down—entering a self-induced trance, if you like—before falling asleep at night. He took care to plant the strong suggestion in his mind beforehand that he would be thirsty during the night, and along with his fast he refrained from taking any water during the previous evening. In another room a glass of water would be placed strategically. By this "need-incapacity" carrot-on-a-string technique, probably enhanced by the various medical drugs he was being treated with at the time, Muldoon succeeded in opening this door without a key.† His method of self-incapacitation, of willed "dying," is still used by occultists in effecting an astral projection, often combined with the so-called "dream method," which was also stumbled across by accident in the 1900's.** This theoretically gives access to a "higher" level than the etheric.

*Sylvan Muldoon and Hereward Carrington, *The Projection of the Astral Body* (Rider, 1951).

†William Seabrook gives an account of such an experiment in his *Witchcraft* (New York, Harcourt, Brace, 1940).

**Oliver Fox, "The Pineal Doorway" and "Beyond the Pineal Doorway," *Occult Review* (1920).

Oliver Fox, a technical college student, realized that he had the ability to become conscious in dreams. He would know that he was dreaming. As a result of this fascinating discovery, he found that he was able to do little tricks in his dreams, such as levitating objects or himself, materializing or dematerializing things, and reducing or expanding things in size. He also found that if he sought to prolong such a dream he would become conscious of his physical body *and* the dream at the same time, in a sort of semiwaking state (overlapping "wavelengths"). He discovered, however, that consciousness of his body included the unpleasant awareness that he was unable to move hand or foot, the familiar incapacity experienced by Muldoon.

By repeated experiment at attaining this state of conscious dreaming, chiefly by carefully remembering dreams on waking and then returning to the same dreams again, Fox managed to perfect a system by which he could enter the mysterious astral world at will. He subsequently evolved a process of concentrating his attention upon what he considered was the area of the brain responsible for these astral experiences: the pineal gland. Since the seventeenth-century French philosopher René Descartes introduced the notion, many occultists have held that the pineal gland was the place where the intangible soul interacts with the physical body. By concentrating upon this "pineal door," as he called it, Fox was able to induce the required state of catalepsy swiftly and then bring on the conscious dream state by forcing his awareness through the area of the pineal trapdoor in his head. This would involve turning his eyes up in his head, "letting go" with all his limbs, and undergoing a short burst of profound concentration.

From the point of view of the Golden Dawn adept, both these methods of astral projection are extremely uncontrolled and clumsy. They might work, but they hurl the projector haphazardly into the astral void without any choice of where he is going. Essentially, the Golden Dawn adept was instructed to perform the following steps when undertaking an astral projection. First, he had to visualize a duplicate of himself clad in his ceremonial robes standing before him, strongly enough to produce an autohypnotic illusion of the same. This step was difficult enough and required long training and constant practice. Having accomplished it, the adept had to suggest to himself that at a given point he would begin viewing his physical body *from the vantage point of this mentally created simulacrum*, a second autohypnotic effect added to the first.

Once he had successfully transferred his consciousness to this illusory "body of light," two courses lay open to him. He could remain active upon the lower etheric level of the astral (as in the instance of Sylvan Muldoon), projecting his consciousness where he wished merely by thinking of the location or person he wished to visit. The journey would then be instantly effected, at least according to the accounts of such adepts as the late Dion Fortune, accompanied by a terrifying sensation similar to a rapid descent in an elevator. Or, alternatively, if the adept wished to contact forces higher up the astral plane, he would "raise his vibrational rate," or shift the setting of his spiritual tuning mechanism by making use of the important memory symbols arranged upon the cabalistic Tree of Life.

Instead of taking potluck, as did Oliver Fox with his lucid dream technique, or visualizing an actual person or place, like Muldoon, the projector would conjure up the visual image (remember the mnemonic "routes"?) of an *imaginary* place. Usually this took the form of a temple furnished with symbols and colors appropriate to the first rung on his tree ladder, which in this instance would be Malkuth, sphere ten, the earth or etheric level. Somewhere in this temple a mysterious gateway would be visualized leading out into darkness. This was the entrance to the "path" leading to the next astral level, that governed by the heavenly body Luna, the Moon.

Each path would introduce a new element of astral phantasmagoria: a tarot trump landscape. The power one would initially encounter as one trod one's first path is shown in modern tarot packs as card number twenty-one, the World. A mysterious figure floating in a vast sea of interstellar darkness, bearing a rod of power in either hand and encircled by a scintillating wreath of green fire, would confront one. Within the wreath the four terrifying heads of the rulers of the four elements, in the form of a bull, a lion, an eagle and an angel would be ablaze at the cardinal points.

By this complex process of producing an astral duplicate of himself, transferring his consciousness to it and finally launching himself into a waking dream world of tarot landscapes and their inhabitants, the Golden Dawn adept sought to climb the heavenly ladder and awaken the powers of the cosmos within himself.

Of course, today's more casual tarot reader, who may know nothing of Rosicrucianism and care less, may find this cabalistic evolution quite superfluous. For him it is enough that the tarot images speak out. But who of us can enjoy the flattened tones of high-fidelity recordings after savoring the full-bodied resonance of stereophonic sound?

The Golden Dawn's traditional method of magical memory training is the means by which the tarot is made to speak out resonantly. The cabalistic accumulations of the nineteenth century are quite irrelevant. The method itself is the key, and it is one similar to the mental exercise students of depth psychology call "free association."

According to the psychologist C. G. Jung, archetypes, images of myth and dream alike, rooted deeply in man's primordial being constantly find expression in our everyday lives but can be discovered most abundantly in the symbolism of the occult sciences, astrology and alchemy. This is equally true of the tarot. Indeed, the tarot seems to have evolved as just such an encyclopedia of magical memory images into which one may dip.

CHAPTER 4

The Old Religion

Although we now know what type of creature the tarot is—namely, a magical memory file—we have yet to see which pagan cults provided the images for the individual cards. To do this we must follow a trail leading through a maze of mythologies. Although some of the legends seem to have been based upon real happenings, rarely do the cults which turned these events into myths remain in existence. Very often all we have left of an entire religion is one of these quaint fairy stories. One extraordinary exception to this rule provides us with a good starting point for our tarot trail.

This was the curious cult of Roman paganism that the nineteenth-century American folklorist Godfrey Leland discovered flourishing in the town of Florence and its outlying districts in 1886.* The chief deity worshiped by adherents of this cult, who called themselves *strege* and *streghoni*—witches and wizards—was one Aradia, said to be the daughter of the classical Moon goddess Diana.

Possibly Aradia is synonymous with the goddess Herodias, worshiped by witches during the Dark Ages according to a tenth-century ecclesiastical tract called the *Canon Episcopi*.

*C. G. Leland, *Aradia, the Gospel of the Witches* (London, David Nutt, 1899) and C. G. Leland, *Etruscan Magic and Occult Remedies* (New York, University Books, 1963).

Aradia appears to have played the part of a mediator between her worshipers and her mother Diana, who was considered to be supreme above all the other gods. "Diana was the first created before all creation; in her were all things; out of herself, the first darkness, she divided herself; into darkness and light she was divided. Lucifer, her brother and son, herself and her other half, was the light," says the Florentine witches' gospel.*

This type of dualistic creation was a specialty of Gnosticism and was particularly frowned upon by the church whenever it appeared in the teachings of heretical sects such as the Albigenses or Manicheans. The Florentine legend goes on to recount how the incarnate Diana descended to earth in pursuit of Lucifer, with whom she had incestuously fallen in love and who had made the earth his home—had "fallen," as the church would say. From the union of Diana and Lucifer all the supernatural beings intermediary between heaven and earth were born—the elves, dwarves, giants, fauns and witches headed by Aradia. It is from Diana that all these supernatural folk learn their magical arts.

This type of legend is by no means original to Florence, however. There are many similar to it in European mythology. Fundamentally they all have the same structure. Two elements, often the Sun and the Moon, or the evening and morning star, predominate. Twin deities proceed from a single, two-sexed parent; one of these twins vanishes or is snatched away, and the other sets off in pursuit. On the surface it appears to be an obvious astronomical myth relating to the rotation of the heavens.

A Nordic account of those fertility gods known as the Vanir tells just such a tale of divine twins. Their primordial parent was called Njörd or Nerthus, a name probably signifying the great Deep. The twins themselves were called Frey and Freyja, meaning simply "the lord" and "the lady," and they took over the duties of their divine parent in running creation. Frey shared all the attributes of the beautiful young dying god Adonis or Tammuz,

*C. G. Leland, *Aradia, the Gospel of the Witches* (London, David Nutt, 1899), p. 18.

Figure 21

whose cult was widely celebrated throughout the Middle East prior to the advent of Christianity; he too vanished into death and darkness. Freyja then set off in search for her lost brother in a chariot drawn by cats, a mode of transport incidentally also adopted by Diana. (See Figures 21 and 22.) In ancient Greek mythology we again run across this story, in a slightly altered form. Hermes, the messenger god, undertakes a search for Persephone, the daughter of Demeter, "Mother Nature." The girl has been carried off by Hades, lord of the underworld, to be his bride in the land of the dead. Due to Hermes' intervention, Persephone is allowed to spend half her days upon earth with her mother and the other half with Hades, thus accounting in the eyes of the Greeks for the division of the year into summer and winter. Summer came when Persephone was dwelling with her mother, winter when she ruled beneath the earth.

A similar Greek story of hide and seek was told of the poet Orpheus, to whose compelling incantations and songs even the stones, trees and animals danced. His beloved Eurydice was

Figure 22

bitten by a snake and also fell into the power of the god of death. Orpheus followed her down to the underworld and won her back with the help of his songs and incantations.

Then there is yet a third Greek story which recounts how the god Dionysus, descending into the land of death, searched for his mother Semele.

All these tales present the ancient idea that death is a place where souls are imprisoned. It is brought out even more clearly in the Greek legend of Theseus and the Minotaur, which illustrates this hide-and-seek theme but in a more complex and less obvious manner.

Pasiphaë, the wife of King Minos of Crete, had given birth to a monster—half man, half bull—known as the Minotaur. It was a carnivorous beast and had to be appeased every year by an offering of men and women from Crete's vassal states. Theseus, the Athenian king's son, volunteered to destroy the Minotaur in its mazelike lair, or labyrinth, constructed especially for it by King Minos' master craftsman Daedalus. He accomplished this with the aid of Minos' daughter, Ariadne. She gave him a thread or, according to another version, a light-giving golden bough lent her by the god Dionysus, which guided the young hero into the terrible maze and out again after he had slain the beast.

This legend seems to contain the elements of an initiation ritual of the Minoan bull cult. The horned god of death dwelling like some large spider in the middle of his mazelike stronghold represents the intricate snares of the underworld; the initiate can only achieve the quest with the aid of a magical thread provided by the beast's daughter-wife Ariadne, whose name may well be of similar derivation to Aradia's.

All of these Greek stories, although now classed as an integral part of classical anthologies of the *Tanglewood Tales* variety, appear to have originally sprung from a culture considerably older than that which furnished the usual legends of the Olympians—the exploits of Zeus and his crew. In Homeric myth the deities of these older cults, even then seen as mysterious and sinister, are referred to as Titans, the children of the original Sky Father Ouranos and Earth Mother Gaia.

An extremely ancient legend which deals specifically with these elder gods and parallels the Aradia creation myth concerns the mysterious race of people known as the Cabiri. It also provides an account of a wonder-working race resulting from the original divine mating, who under another terminology might well be referred to as elves and witches in the manner that Aradia does.

According to the disciples of the Greek philosopher Pythagoras, the Cabiri were the precursors of the Olympian gods. As in the legend of Diana, this race of Titans was spawned from the seed of the oldest gods of all. The ancient hermaphroditic mother goddess Axieros gave birth to, or divided into, a male and a female, Axiokersos and Axiokersa.

The union of Axiokersos and Axiokersa produced the race of Cabiri, headed by one Kadmilos, identified by some as Hermes-Thoth and by others as Dionysus. The Cabiri were named after their reputed place of origin, Mount Kabeiros in Berekyntia.

Apart from being credited with the invention of the alphabet and the discovery of arithmetic and algebra, the Cabiri were thought to possess great powers of sorcery. They could destroy with their glance alone, change their outward appearance and even effect changes in the weather. According to the writer Pausanias, the Cabiri—under their epithet Dactyls (meaning "digits" or "fingers")—were divided broadly into two classes: the females, who were witches who specialized in casting spells, and the males, who were smiths and metalworkers and could effectively break the spells so laid. The magical awe that has always attended the metalworking smith throughout the Western world may be closely connected with them. An ancient Irish charm known as the Lorica (breastplate) of Saint Patrick invokes the aid of God:

> . . . Against incantations of false prophets,
> Against the black laws of paganism
> Against spells of witches, smiths and druids,
> Against all knowledge that is forbidden to the human soul. . . .

The Cabiri specialized in the use of bronze rather than iron. Many of the magical accessories owned by the Olympian gods were said to have been fashioned from this brown metal by Hephaestus, the Cabiri's volcano god: Kronos' sickle, Poseidon's trident, Zeus' thunderbolt, Hades' helmet of invisibility and Aphrodite's girdle, to name but a few.

From Berekyntia the Cabiri migrated to Samothrace, and it was from this island and its neighbors Lemnos and Imbros that legends concerning them first appear to have emanated. During their early wanderings it is said that they came to Crete and colonized it (the name Crete itself derived from "Kurete," another of their titles). Thence they journeyed to Cyprus, then to Rhodes, which received the name "Telchines," from "Telcine," yet another of their aliases.

It is here, according to the poet Ovid,* that they accurately predicted the angry gods would drown out sinful mankind with a great flood, thus tying the legend in with those of Utnapishtim, Noah and Deucalion.

*Ovid, *Metamorphoses*, Ch. 7, v. 367.

The word *kabieroi* may be connected to the Phoenician *qabirim*, meaning "mighty ones." In view of the fact that they were regarded as wonder-workers, this interpretation may have some foundation of truth; they obviously have close links with the Nephelim, an antediluvian race of Titans mentioned in the Kabbalah, who were said to be the offspring of mortal women and fallen angels. This "angelic exile" seems to be yet another version of the underworld-descent story.

The *Book of Enoch*, an apocryphal cabalistic work of the second century B.C., recounts how the angelic "sons of heaven" led by Azazel (Lucifer) left their home among the stars to dwell among mankind, seduced, says the author of the work, by the beauty of the daughters of men. According to the *Zohar*, another ancient cabalistic work, these beings had to assume tangible material bodies in order to descend upon the earth. By terrible mischance—others say at the will of God for having disobeyed his command—they found themselves unable to divest themselves of their material bodies to make the transition back to their own world. Yet another legend maintains that Lucifer lost the jewel—some say a fire ruby, others an emerald—that was bound to his brow in a circlet and in which lay the power of ascending to and descending from the heavenly places. Clearly this legend also has close ties with an Arabic fable current during the Middle Ages concerning Haroot and Maroot, two mighty archangels who as a consequence of their compassion for the frailty of humankind were sent to earth to be tempted. They subsequently succumbed to the charms of Homo sapiens and settled down as rulers of Babylon, where they proceeded to instruct mankind in the arts and sciences.

All these myths deal initially with a divine game of hide and seek. During the rest periods in their chase, the gods who play it find time to instruct mankind in the arts of civilization. The story seems to represent a cycle of sorts: though the gods depart, they will come back again.

Anthropologists have speculated that this cycle undoubtedly derives from that of the cyclic progression of the seasons, the heavenly bodies and the life-span of livestock and humans. But the myths themselves subsequently became responsible for practices which link together such items as Rosicrucian memory systems, the cabalists' Tree of Life and also, as we shall see, tarot cards.

Today these practices are referred to as "shamanic." According to the dictionary, a shaman is a primitive priest, medicine man, or exorcist—that is, someone who commands the gods or ghosts of the dead. The word itself is thought to derive from the Mongolian or Persian, meaning an idolator. However, in actuality there is a considerable practical difference between priestcraft and shamanism. Basically, a shaman can be said to perform his art by rule of thumb, accumulating practical experience of the character of his gods by sending his spirit to visit them in their own abodes while he is in a trance, rather than by the priest's method of merely relying on a blind faith that the invisible world is paying heed to his prayers and invocations. Shamanic power is therefore always attained firsthand rather than simply by belonging to a priesthood. The only true test of a shaman's skill lies in his ability to get results, and this only comes from a personal acquaintance with the spirits he meets on his journeys to the other world.

The novice shaman's first journey to the spirits is made during a state of dissociation usually brought on by fasting in solitude, which may often be aided by self-imposed rigors and tortures. A typical shamanic self-mortification was one of bodily suspension in the air from a beam or post. There is considerable reason to believe that Germanic Odin-worshiping shamans practiced this form of self-initiation by hanging themselves upon the boughs of trees.* The wonder tree Yggdrasil itself meant "the horse of Ygg [Odin]," for Odin was said to have hanged himself upon it to gain magical power and foresight. In a similar manner, the gallows tree in Norse myth was often referred to as the "hanged man's horse." The bodies of those slain upon it were seen as sacrifices to Odin.

*See Mircea Eliade, *Shamanism, Archaic Techniques of Ecstasy* (New York, Bollingen Foundation, 1964), p. 380.

The shaman's spirit journeys are always undertaken for some practical purpose, such as to heal a client or obtain sought-after information. The spirits he visits usually regard him as their chosen mediator or even their adopted son. On occasions they will even possess him, as happens in present-day voodoo ceremonies. For the time being, the shaman thus becomes the divinity himself in the eyes of his flock.

Parapsychologists have theorized that this is what occurs during the spiritualist's trance mediumship. Here a secondary personality is assumed by someone seeking contact with the spirit world or the production of psychic phenomena. This secondary personality or "spirit guide" will usually claim to be the disembodied spirit of some significant holy person such as an Indian rishi, Pawnee medicine man, Greek philosopher or ancient Egyptian priest. From a psychological point of view, the reason for this ploy is an obvious one: by becoming someone else, the medium shifts the responsibility for the ESP or PK phenomena that is (or isn't) about to be produced onto the shoulders of that other person. He also bypasses any of his own personality traits, such as skepticism, which would inhibit the flow of his psi powers. In fact, it is a very effective method of "suspending disbelief." Any myth dealing with the quest for some lost god or supernatural treasure carries these shamanic implications.

The great Mediterranean goddess, known as Ishtar, Astarte, Ininna, Beltis or Cybele, searches the underworld for and regains her beloved son-lover, Tammuz, Baal or Attis. In the north the myth emerges as Frigg searching for Balder or Freyja for Frey. In Egypt it is Isis searching for Osiris. During the Middle Ages the Latin variant of the myth, Venus' search for Adonis, becomes the basis for the legend of Tannhuser. It even creeps into children's fairy tales as a Hans Christian Andersen story: Gerda journeys to the land of perpetual winter, the North Pole, to rescue her beloved brother Kay, who is imprisoned there by the Snow Queen. They are all typically shamanic themes, as is the Florentine witch legend of Diana's pursuit of Lucifer.

And as far as medieval witchcraft is concerned, we have only

to compare the paraphernalia of the shaman with that traditionally ascribed to the witch to realize that they are one and the
same person. The shaman will wear a special caftanlike robe to
work his magic in. His assistants, on the other hand, may wear
no clothes at all. The shaman's robe will almost invariably be
decorated with images of the sun, moon and stars, and sometimes pictures of totem animals and magical signs. This is, of
course, the traditional wizard's garment alongside the female
witch's nudity. The shaman will also wear a cap made of the
whole skin of a small animal, such as a lynx or a brown-owl, as did
the witch's precursors, the druid and the bard. On top of this may
be placed a metal crown from which spring two or three horns—
often those of a stag, buffalo, bull or goat—two on either side,
and sometimes an additional shorter one in the center.* This, of
course, is the traditional horned headdress of the devil.

The caldron is another major magical implement, traditionally used by both shamans and witches. Candidates for shamanic initiation are "boiled" to life in it, a practice also adopted by
the classical witch Medea when rejuvenating Jason's father.

But the instrument par excellence of the shaman's art is his
staff. He uses this chiefly as a hobbyhorse on which to make
magical ascents and descents into the spirit world. Traditionally
it is tipped with a carved horse's head or phallus;† this also
happens to be an excellent description of a traditional witch's
riding staff or "broomstick," like the one ridden by Dame Alice
Kyteler in 1324.** The shamanic staff may be made out of
birchwood or ash wood, and the tree from which it is cut must
remain alive, recalling the witch practice of making a magical
fetish from a mandrake, datura plant or mountain ash. In fact,
this hobbyhorse seems to be a diminutive version of the cosmic
tree itself. In the instance of an ash staff, the shaman is actually
climbing the world tree when he mounts it. Or the staff may
become elongated into a notched climbing pole. The climbing

*Mircea Eliade, *Shamanism, Archaic Techniques of Ecstasy* (New York, Bollingen
Foundation, 1964), pp. 145-80.
†Mircea Eliade, *Shamanism, Archaic Techniques of Ecstasy* (New York, Bollingen
Foundation, 1964).
**Proceedings Against Dame Alice Kyteler* (London, Camden Society Publications,
1843).

or riding is a ritual act performed to induce the required ecstasy and consequent magical journey.

A present-day primitive Siberian shaman among the Ural-Altaian and Buryat peoples will, for instance, accomplish the feat of casting forth his spirit either by descending through the earth in trance to visit Erlik Khan, the lord of the underworld, or by ascending to heaven to obtain information from the celestial gods. To do this he will physically climb the notches cut into a birch pole set in the center of his ritual tent. The top of the pole points toward the Pole Star through the smoke hole above. Each notch in the birch-tree ladder signifies one of the planetary spheres, the highest being those of the Moon, Sun and, topmost, the Absolute.*

The Rosicrucian ascent of the tree of life is likewise simply a development of this basic shamanic practice: like Odin, the adept mounts a tree in search of supernatural wisdom.

Now shamanic doctrine wherever found, whether in ancient Greece or among Navaho Indians, is always presented in the form of a theophany, or Mystery play—in its simplest form, a fairy tale or song. It always begins with the birth of the semidivine hero or heroine, the original shaman, and continues with his worldly trials, loves and triumphs. Halfway through the cycle he experiences catastrophic loss in the form of suffering or death, generally his own or that of a loved one. This is followed by the hero's journey to the other world to confront the spirits responsible for this loss. He comes to terms with them by means of force, cunning or simply flattery, and the victory results in the conferment of magic power or acquisition of the sought-after prize, be it the beloved's or his own soul or some magical treasure like the grail. The hero now returns to the everyday world. His return is always accompanied by rejoicing, for he has conquered the other world. Often this festivity takes the form of an actual elevation of the returning shaman to the status of a god.

This type of story later came to provide the basis for most

*See Mircea Eliade, *Shamanism, Archaic Techniques of Ecstasy* (New York, Bollingen Foundation, 1964).

initiation Mysteries. "Mystery" is a technical term which simply means a supernatural drama or sacred history, usually kept secret and revealed only to devotees of the god at their initiation into his cult. A supernatural drama of this sort also appears quite clearly depicted in the tarot trumps.

Though in typically syncretist fashion the images seem to be drawn from a variety of sources, there is a consistency to the tarot story. A clue to which myth it is taken from may well lie within the word "trump" itself. Nobody is quite sure where this term comes from. It has been associated with the tarots as far back as cartomancers can remember. The word was originally "triumph" and simply meant a victory or a prevailing. The game of tarots already delineated is in fact the old game of "triumphs," or victories. However, the victories are not those won in the card game but are something within the cards themselves. The Latin word from which "triumph" itself derives is *triumphus*, which in turn is drawn from the Greek *thriambos*. Though the Roman *triumphus* finally came to mean any processional pageant in honor of a victorious general as he entered a city,* the Greek *thriambos* leads us to its original, most basic meaning: a processional hymn of the god Dionysus celebrating his triumph over death, rebirth and subsequent apotheosis. The tarot story would then be that of Dionysus, as recounted by his devotees, the disciples of Orpheus.

In the light of this hypothesis, the tarot Fool is quite apparently the innocent child Dionysus himself, who latterly came to be equated with the Sun and Mithras.†

That wandering Asian tribes, such as in later times would be styled "gypsy," could have been responsible for the reintroduction of the Dionysian cult to Greece may not be too much of an assumption. According to the disciples of Orpheus, Dionysus preceded the classical deities. He subsequently returned from Asia to claim his own, as dramatized in the legend of Pen-

---

*For this interpretation of the trumps, see Gertrude Moakley, *The Tarot Cards Painted by Bembo* (New York, New York Public Library, 1966).
†See M. J. Vermaseren, *Mithras, the Secret God*, trans. by T. and V. Megan (London, Chatto and Windus, 1963).

theus.* That the tarot is intimately connected with the gypsies has already been shown.

The lesser trumps (the Juggler, Female Pope, Empress, Emperor, Pope) may represent the "lesser Mysteries," such as those that came to be held at Agrae after their introduction from Asia. The greater trumps would then be the "greater Mysteries" of Eleusis. These Mysteries were four great religious festivals held over the period of two years. They were open to the public and extremely popular in view of the assurance of immortality in an afterlife that they gave the participants. Because the Mysteries shared this in common with early Christianity, the call of the Resurrection cult of Jesus fell on willing ears among the Gentile slaves of the pagan world. From what we can piece together of these rites, during the initial May festival, Hades' abduction of Persephone was celebrated. The mourning of her mother Demeter was celebrated the succeeding autumn. The second May festival celebrated the birth of Dionysus, his life and violent death, followed by his heart in the form of pomegranate seeds being given by Hades to Persephone to eat. This action resulted in the impregnation of Persephone, her establishment as underworld goddess for a third of the year, and the rebirth of Dionysus as Iacchus, all celebrated the following autumn.

That the complex drama of the young god and his mother-sister-bride was enacted in one form or another in the various Mystery-cult centers is fairly certain. That these legends of death and resurrection contributed to the later Messianic stories surrounding Jesus also seems highly likely.

In this way the entire Mystery cycle of the pagan initiate's triumphs came to be paralleled in the Christian myth—Jesus' semidivine parentage, progress through the world of the elements toward the initiation of death, descent into the underworld, defeat of death and final resurrection and ascent into the empyrean. Whether the initiate was Orphic or Eleusinian, Mithraic or Christian, the formula seems to have been identical in

---

*See Euripides, *The Bacchae.*

pattern. In fact, as we shall see, the tarot trumps present a fusion of these cults typical of syncretist thinking.

Because the god or goddess central to the myth had already successfully made his journey through death—Diana had retrieved Lucifer, Freyja Frey, Dionysus Semele, Hermes Persephone, Isis Osiris, Astarte Tammuz and later Christ the lost souls, or "Sophia," so could the initiate also step fearlessly into death. He simply followed in their footsteps, seeing his life, loves, triumphs, failures and final death against the backdrop of this myth. Everything became relevant in its light. He saw himself either as the beloved, saved from death by the wandering deity, or, if he were the hierophant responsible for unfolding the Mystery, as the deity itself.

Thus the picture shown on each tarot trump seems to characterize some particular facet of human experience. Each stage theoretically brings with it fresh understanding of what life is all about. Originally these initiations may have been purely mundane, such as the experience of love. But centuries added to their mystery. To the medieval occultist, the trumps undoubtedly contained all sorts of occult powers, for by their mythological associations many of them shared common symbols with magical notae, which, as we have seen, were talismans in their own right.

CHAPTER 5

The Devil's Picturebook

We shall now explore the tarot trumps in detail.

The Minor Arcana appears to have very little to do with the magical tale woven by the tarots, save in its general connection with the four "virtue" trumps, which I will deal with under their correct headings. The trump sequence that I present here is a tidied-up one. There are many conflicting accounts of the correct order in which the cards should be arranged, each one peculiar to the interpretation that the author favors most. In the following chapters, I have more or less adhered to the widely accepted order of most Italian packs and the so-called Marseilles deck. The earliest known pack, that of Charles VI, is, in fact, unnumbered. However, if we acknowledge the "Mystery" hypothesis, we shall find that the cards tend to fall into natural groups, although a certain amount of diffusion appears to have taken place—such as the spreading out of the elemental cardinal virtues. But so long as we keep the lesser and greater trumps in their correct relative positions at the beginning and end of the sequence, with the Wheel of Fortune and Tree of Initiation standing between them as a pivotal axle, then the archetypal story still remains apparent and the initiate's mnemonic ladder intact.

The Fool

As we saw in the last chapter, the key to the tarot rests in the card known as the Fool (see Figure 23). During the Middle Ages he was known as the Lord of Misrule, but now others more cabalistically inclined call him the Babe in the Abyss. Many people call him simply the Joker. This is what he has ended up as in modern playing card decks.

Figure 23

In early tarot decks you will find him sometimes dressed in penitential white and sometimes in rags. Often he wears feathers stuck in his hair, as in the Bembo deck, or sports a horned or ass-eared jester's cap. These are all that are left of his original horns and asses' ears (see Figure 24).

Dionysus, or Iacchus—the "phosphoros aster" (light-bearing star), as the Greek playwright Aristophanes calls him—was the youngest son of the Olympian Sky Father, Zeus. Some legends alternatively name Hades as his father. In fact, Hades was simply a dark version of the Mighty Thunderer himself, often being referred to as Zeus Katachthonios, the "subterranean Zeus."

Figure 24

Legend tells us that Zeus Katachthonios fathered Dionysus upon his own sister Demeter. At his birth he was found to bear small horns on his forehead like a kid or small calf. According to the legend that attributed fatherhood to Zeus, Hera the All Father's ever jealous celestial wife, sent a band of monstrous Titans to tear the horned child to pieces. They dismembered him into seven portions, which they boiled in a caldron and consumed, although Zeus got possession of the heart. From it he prepared a potion which he administered to the Theban princess Semele, some say the goddess Persephone, causing her to reconceive the young child.

Vengeful Hera, however, ever vigilant, disguised herself as a nurse and persuaded the unlucky Semele to demand that her divine lover reveal himself in all his terrible splendor. In vain Zeus tried to dissuade her, but she persisted in her wish, to her own destruction, as indeed the omniscient All Father knew would be the case. Semele perished, scorched like a moth in a candle flame at the sight of Zeus' terrible radiance. Hera's vengeance seemed complete—but not quite. Before Semele fell into the underworld, the All Father plucked the yet unborn child from her womb and sealed it in his own thigh until it was due to be delivered. At that time upon Mount Nysa he delivered the precious baby into the hands of the god Hermes for instruction and safekeeping.

The horns with which Dionysus was born indicate his links with the young horned animal that was considered a suitable sacrificial offering to the gods in the ancient Mediterranean world. However, not only was he a victim of the hunt but also a hunter in his own right, as his name Zagreus, "the Great Hunter," implies (see Figure 25). In fact, this is his divine father's name also. Just as Persephone was the young alter ego of her mother, Demeter, so was Dionysus the younger version of his father, Zeus Katachthonios.

The Horned Child as Bacchus was said to have bestowed the gift of wine upon mankind—one of the ancient doorways to ecstasy, that mysterious standing outside oneself that is the goal of mystical adventure.

Like his successor Jesus, Dionysus was also an overturner of hidebound traditions and restrictive tyranny. He was the incarnate power of spiritual revolt and rebirth.

His traditions passed into medieval European life despite all the efforts made by the church to stamp them out, and he became known as the Lord of Misrule. The winter festivities of Christmas and Holy Innocents Day were shadows of his old feast days held at Saturnalia. During the time of the pagan amalgamation, Dionysus had been equated with Mithra on the

Figure 25

one hand and the Sun on the other, and his birthday was celebrated at the winter solstice. This is the occasion when the Sun rounds its nadir and returns, reborn from the darkness of the underworld. Jesus' birth had originally been placed at January 5 by the early Christians, but at the suggestion of the more missionary minded it was backdated to December 25 to coincide with the pagan birthday of the Sun.

As late as 1645 a pious Frenchman, Mathurin de Neuré, wrote a letter to "Father" Pierre Gassendi, a skeptical mathematician and philosopher famous for his refutation of Aristotle, complaining of the ecclesiastical buffoonery at the Monastery of Cordeliers in Antibes on Holy Innocents Day. Mock bishops had been elected, obscene songs sung, "black masses" celebrated at the altar using cakes and sausage instead of the consecrated host, and games played instead of solemn ceremonials.

The Lord of Misrule also showed his presence at the winter

"Feast of the Ass," when a representation of the Madonna and Child was led into cathedral sanctuaries seated on an ass and a burlesque litany was sung with "hee-haws" being chanted by the congregation as responses.

And, strangely enough, these practices were officially acceded to by the church well into the Middle Ages. There was a time and a place for everything, even anarchy. Early Christianity, taking over from its pagan forebears, was compelled to go along with this if it wished to maintain a grip on its converts. All that is left of the fool's festivities in our modern calendar is Christmas and April 1.

Boy bishops and burlesque masses aside, the Fool himself played a much larger part in medieval life than merely to ape ecclesiastical ceremonies prior to Lent. In fact, he was often an integral part of every feudal court, attaining considerable fame in later times.* Great lords often found place for a fool in their households. There he held an honored position, and his job, apart from merely keeping his master entertained, was to remind him that, like Caesar, he too was only human and open to error. Theoretically the poor fool was the one person at court immune from retribution for quips at his master's expense. However, all too often he became the butt for cruel jokes for, like Dionysus, he was also a scapegoat.

In older tarot decks the Fool is often portrayed as ragged and unkempt, spurning the ways of the world. The Mantegna tarot of 1484 shows him simply as a beggar, who, like the Indian sannyasi, has nowhere to lay his head, nothing and no one to call his own. In later decks he appears in complete jester's panoply with cap and bells and bladder.

He is equated by Rosicrucian cabalists with aleph, the first letter of the Hebrew alphabet, meaning the beginning of all. However, Florentine Minchiate decks place him at the end of the trump series after the World. Alpha and omega would perhaps be more accurate. These practical occultists also use the image of the Fool as a magical nota in the following manner.

*Such as the celebrated *Matello, the fool of Isabella d'Este, Marchioness of Mantua.*

According to old legends, Dionysus was the reborn younger image of his father, in one branch of the myth, as we have seen, held to be the subterranean god of death, Hades himself. Now one of Hades' chief attributes was the power of invisibility. He owned a helmet made by Hephaestus which conferred this power upon him, and many of the representations of him in Greek art portray him thus, with head turned backward. Hence his title Hades, which itself means "the invisible making." His son Dionysus also retained this characteristic.

According to the Neoplatonists, the Egyptian version of the divine child, Harpocrates, who was portrayed in ancient art as an infant seated upon a lotus with thumb and forefinger to lips, symbolized both the secrecy incumbent upon initiates into the Mysteries and the magical power of withdrawal and concealment accorded to them by the gods in time of need. During the period of the pagan amalgamation, the divine child of one pantheon was often linked with that of another. Thus it is hardly surprising that the invisible Dionysus born in the underworld on December 25 came to be linked in occultists' minds with the child Harpocrates. In modern cabalism he is called the Babe in the Abyss (underworld).

Therefore, when a cabalist wishes to invoke the power of protection and invisibility, he meditates upon the image of the tarot Fool, often imagining himself in the form of the figure portrayed in his deck of tarots!

Often this "assumption of the god form" is combined with a ritual. Whether there is any occult virtue in the actual objects used in these spells or whether it is simply the game itself which sets the deep mind in motion is a much debated point among occultists.

According to those who have studied this art of "invisibility," the process is one of fascination—that is, methods of deluding the senses of the onlookers. "Unnoticeability" would theoretically be a better term, for the victims of the spell, far from seeing through the practitioner, are said simply to refuse to acknowledge his presence among them in the way that a hypnotized subject does when informed that he is unable to see a certain object in the room.

Both of these traditional spells make use of talismans which are "charged" with one's intention and then carried as a sort of broadcasting unit for a blanket of protective darkness.

Two talismans of invisibility

In modern times the name for this talisman has been abbreviated to simply a Lucky Hand. It used to be known as the Hand of Glory. The derivation of the term itself is interesting. Stemming from the Greek *Mandragora*, it passed into old medieval French *grimoires* as *Main de gloire* (Hand of Glory). However, the talisman described was not in this instance a mandrake root but rather the root and sprouts of the midsummer fern, Dryopteris filix-mas. According to an alternative medieval tradition made famous by R. H. Barham in *The Ingoldsby Legends*, the talisman was an actual hand severed from the body of a hanged criminal and pickled in zimort, saltpeter, salt and peppercorns. This grisly trophy was then cured over a fire of fern and vervain. The grease exuded was retained, mixed with sesame oil and twisted with a wick into a taper which was attached to the knuckles of the hand. When lit and borne aloft, this bizarre candle was said to cause all doors of a house to come unlocked in its eerie light and all occupants within to be cast into a deep sleep. The boon companion of the thief! (See Figure 26.)

The midsummer fern variety is, however, the older tradition and, needless to say, is more widely adhered to than the other. At dark of the Moon you should trace a circle clockwise around the fern and yourself with a new knife. Then dig up the plant carefully, using your hands as much as possible for the task. As you remove the plant you must "ask its permission," carefully stating that you intend to make a Hand of Glory which will serve you as a shield of darkness and protection.

Trim the fern fronds with your knife now, so that only five of them remain sprouting from the top. These are the basis for the five fingers. The stem provides the wrist. As you whittle

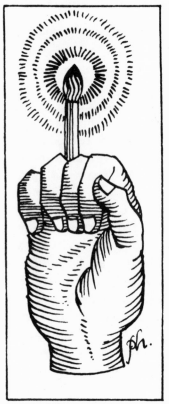

Figure 26

away at the hand, trying to make it as lifelike as possible, chant a traditional invisibility spell, such as the following:

> Almiras, Master of Invisibility!
> I conjure thee and thy ministers
> Cheros! Maitor! Tangedum!
> Transedim! Suvantos! Abelaios! Bored!
> Belamith! Castumi! Dabuel!
> By that through which all things have their being!
> And by Saturiel! Harchiel! Daniel!

Beniel! Assimonem!
That thou and thy Ministers render me invisible
To all eyes that I shall indicate!
Sceaboles! Arbaron! Elohi!
Elmigith! Herenobulcule!
Methe! Baluth! Timayul!
Teveni! Yevie! Ferete!
Bacuhaba! Guvarin!
By the empire which ye exert over us,
Fulfil this work that I may pass invisible
To whom I wish!

To complete this spell, dry the hand on midsummer's eve over a fire on which vervain or verbena leaves have been cast, again repeating the invisibility charm. Hang the completed talisman near your hearth at home until you wish to use it.

Alternatively, on the day and hour of Saturn (Saturday at 1 A.M., 8 A.M., 3 P.M., or 10 P.M.) draw a circle clockwise around yourself with your new knife. Starting within this circle, mold some wax into an image of the person for whom the spell is being cast and incise his or her name on it with your knife.

Now, taking a few drops of water, "baptize" the image with the subject's name. Then slice the top of the head off the figurine and inscribe the symbols shown in diagram A on the exposed surface before replacing the wax as before. You are here symbolically engraving darkness notae upon the brain of the subject. Then take the skin of a frog or a toad and write on it the words "Hele, Hele, Hele," accompanied by the runes shown in diagram B. The words themselves mean "thrice hidden"; the last two symbols probably refer to the first and last

Diagram A

letters of the Greek alphabet, alpha and omega. The frog skin, a
Saturnine object, is often used in invisibility magic, legendary
"caps of invisibility" generally being made from them.

Finally, press a single hair from the head of someone you
know to be well disposed to the bearer, such as yourself, into

Diagram B

the soft wax. Then pass the image through some sweet-smelling
incense smoke, chanting as you do the cabalistic invisibility
spell:

> Metatron, Melekh, Beroth, Noth,
> Vennibeth, Mach and all ye,
> I conjure
> thee O figure of wax by the Living One
> and by the virtue of these characters and
> words, that thou holdest the eyes of all
> beholders, and render him who carries
> thee invisible whenever he beareth thee
> with him!

Complete the operation by wrapping the image in the frog
skin and placing it in a small pine box for safekeeping. When the
owner wishes to make use of it, he must conceal it somewhere
on his left side.

When the Fool pops up on a tarot spread, you know an
element of anarchy has entered the picture, for traditionally he

represents the irrational, the undetermined—the somehow mysteriously structured chaos which seems to lie at the root of all existence. To the dyed-in-the-wool materialist he will represent a total breakdown in order, absolute entropy, on the one hand, and maybe that "creeping sludge of occultism" which masks the face of madness for him, on the other.

In most decks, however, he is generally left unnumbered or counted as zero. He is the cosmic cipher, the unmarshalable, archetypal square peg, the existential everyman, nonpartisan, nonaligned and "wild," as the poker term has it. The Italians say colloquially: *Esser come il Matto nel tarocchi* (to be like the tarot Fool)—all over the place, at home everywhere and nowhere. The divine bum.

The Juggler

Entitled in modern decks the Magician or the Magus, this card originally showed a fairground huckster in the process of either selling trinkets or performing a sleight-of-hand trick. Alternatively, in some cards he is telling a fortune! (See Figures 27 and 29.)

Closely linked to the Fool, he is all that remains of the classical god Mercury. Mercury, or in Greek Hermes, was another son of Zeus, the All Father, this time born of the gentle nymph Maia. Thus he was the elder half brother of Dionysus, who was placed in his care as soon as he was born.

Hermes was above all else eloquent. As our word "mercurial" implies, he was a person able to wriggle in and out of situations with considerable ease. He was also a deceitful flatterer and a nightly prowler. Images of him known as hermae were erected in his honor in ancient Greece at crossroads, for besides being the god of thieves, he was also the protector of travelers, the prototype of Saint Christopher.

One of the first pranks of the young god was to steal the Sun god Apollo's cattle. When caught in his crime, Hermes successfully squirmed out of the embarrassing situation by bestowing on the angry Sun god a seven-stringed lyre he had made from a tortoise shell. Apollo was delighted by the gift and swiftly forgot his annoyance at the young thief's impudence. Moreover, not only did he forgive him, but he also bestowed gifts upon him in turn: the power of divination—not prophecy, for only Apollo himself could know the will of the All Father—and the offices of guide of souls to the underworld and messenger of the gods. Thus Hermes, apart from his patronage of thieves, came also to represent the *Kerux*, messenger, who led the candidate for the Mysteries into the presence of the gods. Hence the card's alternative name the Magus, the title of the head of a Mithraic

Mystery community. The costume of such a magus usually consisted, according to the ancient writer Hegemon, of a red garment surmounted by a blue mantle, a red pointed cap, and a ring borne on the right hand. In the same hand he also clasped an ebony staff of office.

Figure 27

This pointed, Phrygian cap may have been derived from an ancient herdsman's headgear like the one worn by Mithra himself (see Figure 30). Many old representations of Hermes show him wearing this cap, as do early Renaissance tarot Jugglers (see Figure 29). The broad-brimmed cap of maintenance seen in most modern versions of this card is undoubtedly formed from the usual medieval misinterpretation of the classical winged helmet of Mercury (see Figure 28). The rod which he carries may be either a representation of the caduceus, his magical sleep-inducing heraldic wand of office, or simply a version of the magician's ebony staff.

Mercury, the Latin name, derives from the words *merx* or *mercator* and implies one who is concerned with barter and selling. Thus he is the archetypal wheeler-dealer and purveyor of information, as well as priestly initiator and psychopomp.

Closely associated in spirit with the southern Hermes is the northern god Odin and his mischievous alter ego Loki. Both are sorcerers and cunning-men, and one of Odin's chief functions was to guide the dead.

It is from the name of the knavish god Loki that our word "luck" derives. The English witch-king William Rufus used to take oaths upon "the face of Lucca," and the belief in Loki has lingered on in England to this day. An old Lincolnshire charm for banishing disease performs the required magical action thrice with the words:

> . . . Once for God!
> Once for Wod! [Woden = Odin]
> And once for Lok! [Loki]

The practice of saying "once for luck" at the end of counting out as an appeasement to the god of chance or mischance may well derive from this.

The character of the archetypal mischief maker passed into medieval make-believe in a variety of forms. As "the vice" in old morality plays he was represented as the devil's invisible boon companion, whose function was to belabor other unsuspecting players mirthfully with his "slapstick" (whence our comedy term). He was a poltergeist, in fact, as we shall shortly see. He was also known as Herlequin, the Devil's Messenger, a character similar to the Faust Mephistopheles, who in later Italian and French *Commedia dell arte* plays became Arlecchino or Harlequin, complete with typical multicolored mercurial finery. The stylish nineteenth-century diamond-shaped patches evolved via triangular ones set in a black background, from an initial costume of haphazard multicolored motley.

As the archetypal trickster, the Juggler is also, of course, a great prattler. In the Milanese Italian dialect, the word *bagatt*

Figure 28

means a gossip, and *pagad or bagatto,* the Italian titles for the Juggler, probably derive from this term.

Occasionally, as in the Mantegna tarot, the Juggler is pictured as a gypsy cobbler or artisan instead of a fairground mountebank. This mischievous cobbler image is a familiar one throughout Celtic, Norse and Roman traditions, with their lore of leprechauns, artisan elves and *folletti*—all that is left, maybe, of the aboriginal metalworking little people. You will recall that the Cabiri were thought by the Orphic initiates to have been led by Kadmilos, identified by some as Hermes.

Like the mysterious satyrlike incubi that were rumored to inhabit the great forests of Europe during the Dark Ages and like their German cousins the poltergeists, "noisy spirits," they were often represented as semianimal, sometimes horned, sometimes fox-tailed, but always phallic and indecent.

The English version of the trickster imp is Puck, Shakes-

LE BATELEVR

Figure 29

peare's goblin from *A Midsummer Night's Dream*. Shakespeare represented him as the messenger of the elven king and queen of the wood, Oberon and Titania. This is quite consistent with his ancestry. "Hood," "Hud" or its diminutive "Hudikin" is yet another title for the trickster. Under this name he is very aptly described by the Elizabethan writer Reginald Scot as a "... very familiar devil, who will do nobody hurt, except he receive injury; but he cannot abide that, nor yet be mocked ..."*

Like all elvenfolk, the trickster responded best to gentleness and friendship. In England if you sought his help rather than hindrance, you invoked him by his name Goodfellow.

In Florentine witchcraft, his help is invoked by calling upon him as *follettino rosso*, Little Red Spirit or Goblin, the mischievous attendant of the goddess Diana. He is conjured into a

*Reginald Scot, "Discourse Concerning Devils," in *The Discouverie of Witchcraft* (London, 1665).

small round of stone, which should be thrown up in the air and caught three times and then kept as an amulet to ensure love and payment of debts:

> Spirit of good omen,
> Who art come to aid me,
> Believe I had great need of thee.
> Spirit of the Red Goblin
> Since thou hast come to aid me in my need,
> I pray of thee do not abandon me;
> I beg of thee to enter now this stone,
> That in my pocket I may carry thee,
> And so when anything is needed by me,
> I can call unto thee; be what it may
> Do not abandon me by night or day.
>
> Should I lend money unto any man
> Who will not pay when due, I pray of thee,
> Thou the Red Goblin, make him pay his debt!
> And if he will not and is obstinate,
> Go at him with thy cry of "Brie-Brie!"
> And if he sleeps, awake him with a twitch,
> And pull the covering off and frighten him!
> And follow him about where'er he goes.
>
> So teach him with thy ceaseless "Brie-Brie!"
> That he who obligation e'er forgets
> Shall be in trouble till he pays his debts.
> And so my debtor on the following day
> Shall either bring the money which he owes
> Or send it promptly; so I pray of thee
> O my Red Goblin, come unto my aid!
> Or should I quarrel with her whom I love,
> Then, spirit of good luck, I pray thee go
> To her while sleeping—pull her by the hair,
> And bear her through the night unto my bed!
> And in the morning, when all spirits go
> To their repose, do thou, ere thou return'st
> Into thy stone, carry her home again,
> And leave her there asleep. Therefore, O Sprite!

Figure 30

I beg thee in this pebble make thy home!
Obey in every way all I command.
So in my pocket thou shalt ever be,
And thou and I will ne'er part company!*

The magical images of Mercury enumerated by the wizard Agrippa in his *Fourth Book of Occult Philosophy* contain many of the symbols shown in the harlequin versions of the Juggler trump in addition to the Phrygian cap or winged helmet. ". . . A dog . . . a magpie . . . a garment of many colors; a staff; a short wand . . ."

Agrippa adds that the traditional sign indicating the presence of mercurial spirits is that the conjuror becomes gripped with an unreasoning horror and fear—the traditional panic exhibited in the presence of the mischievous trickster! Hermes and Pan have always been very closely linked in myth, often as father and son.

*C. G. Leland, *Aradia, or the Gospel of the Witches* (London, David Nutt, 1899), pp. 27-28.

The other symbols are equally appropriate. The dog is an animal traditionally associated with Hermes, probably through his associations with another psychopomp, the dog-headed Egyptian mortuary god Anubis. The rod and the staff have been used from time immemorial as emblems of the office of soothsaying.

In fact, all methods of casting lots and reading omens come under the jurisdiction of the trickster, tarot divination not least of all. Medieval occultists often used methods of divination involving the four elements—earth, air, fire and water—as a medium for the omen. Divinations by earth, "geomancy," would use a flat box of sand in which lines of dots would be arbitrarily formed. From these lines omens would then be read.

On the other hand, if the sorcerer felt more at home working with another element, he might use one of the following spells, which can be classed under the headings of pyromancy, hydromancy and aeromancy.

Pyromancy

To divine by fire, state your question and cast powdered frankincense onto red-hot coals, so that it ignites. As it does, make the sign of the horned hand over the coals: either first, second and third fingers folded to palm, thumb and little finger extended, or forefinger and little finger extended, second and third clenched with thumb; both methods were used.

Chant the following words:

> Fire, Fire, holy Fire,
> Unto Fortune I aspire!
> I await a sign from thee
> That my prayers answered be!

Alternatives to powdered frankincense are a dry briar branch, dry poppy seeds, a dry stem of vervain, dry jasmine flowers or a dry branch of laurel. If you use the latter, the nature of your question should be scratched on the leaves with a pencil or pen.

BAD OMENS:

1. The flame is smoky and dark
2. The flame crackles and spits
3. The flame is cleft into two prongs
4. The material refuses to ignite
5. The smoke hangs in a low pall
6. The flame bends over to one side – a sign of impending sickness or difficulty
7. The flame is suddenly extinguished –disaster!

GOOD OMENS:

1. The fire ignites speedily
2. The smoke is scarce, and what little there is ascends in a thin, steady spire
3. The fire burns silently
4. The flame refuses to ignite
5. The flame maintains a cone shape
6. The flame splits into three prongs—success guaranteed!

Flames crackling from side to side are said to presage a visit from friends or relatives. Should the blaze spit out at you, to avert the evil you should immediately spit back at it!

As you will see if you ever try the ingredients for yourself, some are more disaster-prone than others. No doubt this once proved of great value to the less scrupulous village witch!

Hydromancy

In addition to requiring a bowl of water, most hydromantic spells make use of an additional substance such as oil, molten wax or molten lead, which forms patterns when cast into the cold water. These patterns are then scrutinized and omens are read from them according to the intuition of the diviner.

When you wish to divine with wax—ceroscopy or ceromancy,

it is sometimes called—simply melt the wax in a brass ladle (the metal of Mercury), and after briefly asking the god your question, pour the molten liquid into a bowl of cold water. Molten lead may also be used, but the spell is more complex.

Take two new candles and tie a piece of red thread around each of them. Light them at midnight and proceed to melt a small amount of soft lead in your brass ladle or a little fireclay crucible. Into the molten liquid throw three rose seeds, three nettle leaves, two rue leaves and three cumin seeds. Ask Mercury your question and pour the lead into your waiting vessel of cold water.

BAD AUGURY:

If the wax forms a long string or "river" this implies a negative answer to your question. The entire contents of the bowl, water, and lead or wax should immediately be thrown onto an enemy's doorstep or into his backyard!

GOOD AUGURY:

If the molten mass forms itself into a flower-shaped spray or "fountain" a good outcome is assured and the congealed lump should be tied up in a bag of red cloth as an amulet and kept safely until after the happy event has taken place.

Aeromancy

Aeromancy, the branch of divination concerning predictions made by means of the signs of the sky, strictly speaking encompasses the entire art of astrology as well as the field of primitive weather lore. Many instances of the latter have passed into folk traditions, such as old rhymes as "Red sky at night, shepherds' delight Red sky in the morning, shepherds' warning!"

Starlore aside—it would require a book to itself—the chief airy portents by which the ancients divined coming events were the appearances of comets, falling stars and flights of birds. In antiquity a comet was thought to be a "fiery exhalation" from the heavens and was often taken to presage the death of a great man. Falling stars or meteorites were, however, held to be lucky. "Wish upon a falling star . . ." goes the old rhyme. If you could utter the wish to yourself before the elusive streak of light vanished, your wish was bound to come true, provided you obeyed the primary maxim of witchcraft: "Tell no one."

Meteorites or siderites, star stones, were in early times confused because of their iron content with the mysterious mineral magnetite or lodestone, naturally occurring magnetic iron ore. They actually have very little in common save for a loose association of ideas. However, lodestones were and still are held by many to possess great "luck attracting" and prophylactic properties. Originally this was also true of iron found within meteorites, and it was often used for amulets.

Divining by means of flights of birds, sometimes referred to as ornithomancy, was an equally popular method of aerial divination, more so even than astrology, stemming from a time before such complex sciences evolved. In Northern Europe magpies, jackdaws and crows were the favorite birds, all talkative and acquisitive by nature—typically mercurial, in fact! In Italy, the redcap, wild goose and iynx were the southern variants.

Magpies' blood was called for in that old textbook of sorcery the *Key of Solomon* for making a magical knife, or "bolline." This was considered a mercurial spell. On the other hand, the wing feathers of goose and crow were needed to manufacture the consecrated "pens of art" used to draw talismans and pentacles and write the text of the magical rituals in the *Liber Spirituum*, Book of Shadows. This was also mercurial magic.

The following well-known children's rhyme contains remnants of ornithomantic lore. Depending on the number of magpies you saw, so accordingly would the fates deal with you in the future:

> One for sorrow
> Two for mirth
> Three for a wedding
> Four for a birth

One's unlucky,
Two's lucky,
Three's health,
Four's wealth,
Five's sickness,
Six is death!

Two crows, Hugin and Munin—"Thought" and "Memory"—
were the constant companions of Odin, the Nordic Hermes.
They flew far and wide throughout the nine worlds clustered
around the world tree, gathering information from living and
dead, gods, giants or elves, which they would then whisper in
their master's ear as they perched on his shoulder. The old
divination rhyme which has come down to us concerning flights ·
of crows and jackdaws has as many variants as the magpie one:

Five for silver
Six for gold
Seven for a secret that's never been told!

The appearance of the Juggler in a tarot spread implies the
application of some form of skill, cunning, dexterity or even
trickery. Depending on how the card is placed, it may prove to
the querent's advantage or disadvantage. It may also portend an
introduction to something new, for the Juggler is a psychopomp
as well as merchant and master thief.

The Empress

. . . Nevertheless it should not be omitted that some evil women, converted back to Satan's allegiance and seduced by the deceptions and illusions of demons, believe and profess that they ride out by night on beasts with Diana or Herodias the pagan goddess and an innumerable number of women, and cover great distances in the silence of the night, and on certain nights are called to this service . . .

Figure 31

So reads the *Canon Episcopi*, a collection of injunctions against sorcery written some time around A.D. 900 by a certain Regino, Abbot of Prüm. It is one of the significant documents which bridge the gap between classical paganism and the practices of Leland's witches in the nineteenth century.

The mysterious figure known as the Empress in modern tarot packs represents this pagan goddess (see Figure 31). Both comparative religion and Jungian psychology refer to her broadly as the Earth Mother, Mother Nature. She is the mother of Dionysus.

When latter-day syncretic paganism came under the direct fire of the Christian Church around the fourth century A.D., the mother goddesses of various pantheons had already been linked as different aspects of one another. Thus, in the south, Gaia, Rhea and Demeter were seen as Greek manifestations of Roman Tellus, Ops and Ceres, or Cybele, the Asian mountain mother (see Figure 32). In the north their cults were mirrored in those of Nerthus, Frigg and Freyja.

Essentially, the Earth Mother was seen as patroness of all growth and fertility and the mistress of all motherhood. All young defenseless things were under her protection.

Many legends were told of her. Most of them revolve around her search for a loved one of some sort—the eternal shamanic theme which we examined in the preceding chapter. Demeter searches for her abducted daughter Persephone, Ishtar for her lover Tammuz, Cybele for Attis. In the north, Freyja searches for Frey and Frigg for Balder. She is destined to wander the earth, either on foot or in her chariot drawn by mountain cats. In some variants of the story the place of the lost lover is taken by an object. For the Norse goddess Sif it was her golden tresses which were stolen; for Freyja, her precious elven necklace Brisingamen, pilfered by that ever-present troublemaker Loki.

In a different branch of this same myth, Loki contrives the death of the goddess's beloved, in this instance Balder the Beautiful, a northern version of Dionysus or Osiris.

Thus we see that as well as being a goddess of life and joy, she is also a sorrowing one, a Mater Dolorosa periodically mourning the death of her beloved: always the lot of women who see their menfolk go off to spill their blood in wars. It was always to the mother that prayers were offered for grace and healing, and this tradition passed into the Christian Church in the worship of the Virgin Mary.

The Mediterranean worship of the goddess figure appears to stem from a very early age, possibly Bronze or before, when the leadership of the family unit may well have been vested in the mother and grandmother rather than in the male side of the line. Such a matriarchal pattern of life is still widely manifest in the East to this day, especially in Greece and Asia Minor. Though father is the titular head, it is mother who rules the roost.

In Greece the mysteries of the great goddess were celebrated at Eleusis in the cult of Demeter. This was the place where the goddess had been made welcome by Celeus and Metaneira, during her sorrowful search for Persephone. Queen Metaneira entrusted her baby son Demophoön to Demeter's care and, if it had not been for Metaneira's meddling interference, Demeter would have bestowed the gift of immortality upon the young prince. ". . . I swear the great oath of the gods, by the water of the Styx, that I would have made thy dear son into an immortal, who would have remained eternally young, and I would have won for him imperishable renown . . ."*

Instead of this, the goddess taught the followers of King Celeus the sacred rites by which she should be worshiped, which guaranteed the friendliness of her daughter Persephone, queen of the underworld, after death.

Among the plants Demeter held most sacred were corn, barley and mint. The sacramental potion consumed by candidates for her Eleusian Mysteries consisted of barley water stirred with a sprig of fresh Mentha pulegium—usually translated as "mint," though in all probability some variety of pennyroyal herb. The corn, of course, provided the staple diet of her worshipers. In fact the Earth Mother is always considered to be concerned with matters of nourishment and health in whatever place she is worshiped, as evidenced by a quaint Saxon charm

*C. Kerenyi, *The Gods of the Greeks* (N. Y. Evergreen, 1960).

Figure 32

against the dropsy, a disease thought to have been caused by the attack of a water elf who could be successfully suppressed if conjured with the words: *Eorthe the onbere eallum hier mihtum ond maegenum*! ("May Earth bear on thee with all her might and main!")

The Roman sufferer from pains in the feet also called upon the kindly earth, chanting thrice nine times: *Terra pestem teneto; salus hic maneto*! ("Earth, bear thou the pain; health in my feet remain.")

In Roman times the lady's Mysteries were chiefly celebrated in the cults of Vesta and the Bona Dea, Good Goddess, though they later devolved into the orgiastic rites of lewd minor goddesses like Volupia, Strenia and Stimula and were accordingly suppressed. Closely connected with her worship were the cults of minor Italic vegetation goddesses like Rhea Silvia, Diana Nemorensis and Flora.

By medieval times the worship of the Earth Mother had degenerated into folklore, giving rise to agricultural beliefs in various old women and corn mothers.* A very few fragments of it remained in cult form, the goddess being secretly worshiped under such names as Habondia, deriving from the Latinized Dame Abunda, Lady of Plenty, Diana, or other regional names such as Holda, Nocticula or Bensozia.

The wild ride to worship mentioned in the *Canon Episcopi* was not restricted to women, however; men also participated. Neither were the mounts always horses—the canon expressly uses the word "animals." In Italy the steed was often rumored to be the large cat sacred to Diana, in Spain the goat, while in Celtic countries the hare was considered a favorite. In the public mind, however, the shamanic riding pole came to be considered the usual witch steed, following the pattern set by Dame Alice Kyteler, who at her trial for witchcraft in 1324 was accused of possessing a staff on which she merrily "ambled through thick and thin, when and in what manner she listed, after having greased it with the ointment . . ."

The legend of Tannhäuser portrays the goddess as specifically anti-Christian, as did *Aradia.†* As Venus, the Roman Aphrodite, she inhabits the inside of a mountain, where time moves·at a slower pace than in the outer world and where if a mortal should stray he ages a day there for every year outside. Venus is seen as being in direct conflict with the Christian Church, and it is her great delight, like Circe's, to lure innocents such as Tannhäuser into her enchanted realm to the damnation of their souls.

With the advent of the Renaissance, artists and scholars, many of them drawn to occult pursuits, were among the first to take advantage of the lost pagan treasures that were being once again brought to light.

Vincenzo Cartari, an Italian scholar writing for sculptors at

---

*Sir James Frazer, *The Golden Bough* (London, Macmillan, 1922).

†C. G. Leland, *Aradia, or the Gospel of the Witches* (London, David Nutt, 1899), pp. 4-5.

the end of the sixteenth century, gives a description of the image of the goddess Ops, the Italian Earth Mother. The sources he drew upon were ancient and could well have been those that furnished the Empress tarot trump with part of its symbolism:

> . . . She wore upon her head a circlet of towers, because the circumference of the Earth is, like a circlet, full of cities, castles and villages. The robe is woven of green plants and hemmed with leafy boughs thus signifying the trees, plants and herbs which cover the earth. She bears a scepter in her hand. . . . Lions draw [her chariot] .*

Here again we encounter the cat-drawn chariot theme of Diana, Freyja and Cybele.

Many early tarots show the Empress in the costume of a Byzantine ruler such as Theodora, indicating the influence of Eastern Orthodox Christianity, which the cards first came in contact with. The tower-shaped crown preserves its shape throughout, however.

Behind the Empress archetype lurk all those mortal representatives of the goddess, great queens of antiquity such as Hatshepsut, Semiramis, Dido, Cleopatra, and even Theodora herself—all of them regarding themselves as mothers to their respective empires.

When she appears within a card layout, she is said to presage great fruitfulness and productivity or, if badly placed, a frittering away of energy, vacillation or overindulgence. Hers is a card of great beneficence. But too much beneficence can lead to satiety and stagnation, which is one of the interpretations of the card when reversed.

*Vincenzo Cartari, *Le Imagini colla sposizione degli dei degli antichi* (Venice, 1571, Marcolini), pp. 204-6.

The Emperor

In medieval talismanic magic, notae of crowned imperial figures were used as means of attracting honor and wealth and aiding men in business transactions.

The *Picatrix,* an ancient Arabic *grimoire* of sorcery drawn from Gnostic-pagan sources, advocates the use of a nota consisting of the solar image of a crowned, enthroned king robed in gold, with a terrestrial globe under his feet and a raven perched on his forearm close to his breast. This image, the manual instructs, should be etched on a ruby or balas stone, while the Sun is in the first face (ten degrees) of Leo in the ascendant. This means that the magic act is to be performed at dawn at a time and place where the zodiacal sign Leo is in the ascendant—just rising above the horizon. Such an image would render men " . . . invincible and honorable, and help to bring their business to a good end, and to drive away vain dreams; also to be prevalent against fevers and the plague . . . "

The talismanic figure on the Emperor trump is, like its mate, very often depicted in the ceremonial dress of a mid-European archduke or Holy Roman Emperor. Or he could well be the charismatic Carolingian Emperor of the West, Charlemagne himself (see Figure 33).

If the Empress represents the female side of nature then the Emperor undoubtedly symbolizes the male side. In primitive religion, this notion of divine paternalism was often portrayed by giving the god a pair of horns like a male animal; here we undoubtedly have the origin of the shamanic helmet.

The thread of a horned, patriarchal god can be picked up in fragmented form in England in medieval legends of Herne the Hunter and the Green Man. They may well be one and the same person.

Herne, the antlered huntsman, was thought to hunt the souls

Figure 33

of the dead across the night skies and was said to make his home in the hidden reaches of Windsor Forest. The horned, leafy face of the Green Man appears carved into the woodwork of many pre-Reformation churches of England. The Arthurian tale of Sir Gawain's encounter with the undying Green Knight may well be a medievalized account of one of his rites.

But the horned god's ancestry goes back much further than the Dark Ages. The worship of the Celtic divinity Cernunnos was widely prevalent throughout Europe before the Roman conquest (see Figure 34). Representations generally show him possessing curling ram's horns or deer's antlers (see Figure 35). His Celtic name "Cernunnos," with its variants of Cerne and Herne, seem also to signify as much, probably stemming from the word *cerna,* meaning horn.

In classical paganism, the most well-known horned god was Pan. Apart from being the deity of shepherds, this goat-footed god was also the god of hunting, and hunters owed their success or failure to him. According to Theocritus, they would scourge a statue of the god if they had been disappointed in the chase. Many stories were told of Pan's loves, most of them unhappy, typified by that of the nymph Syrinx who turned herself into a reed to escape the embraces of the dark god. His greatest love was, however, for the Moon goddess Selene, in later times identified with Diana. He accomplished her seduction, according to one legend, only after disguising himself in pure white sheepskins. Shakespeare's tale of Oberon and Titania

Figure 34

reproduces this myth in an almost unrecognizably garbled form.

In classical art Pan was often portrayed in the company of the Asian goddess Cybele and the god Dionysus, showing him to be a primitive earthly version of the All Father, as his name Pan, "all-encompassing," suggests. He was closely associated with the phallic god Priapus, whose power was invoked by means of beneficial amulets of rearing and winged phalli (see Figure 36).

These were common both during pagan times and the Dark Ages. The phallus is the All Father's obvious symbol, even as the vagina is that of the Earth Goddess. He is the god of the cosmic tree itself and, strange as it might seem, versions of his flowering rod are still raised at various seasons of the year in Europe, namely at Christmas and May Day! Philip Stubbes, a noted Puritan writer of the reign of Queen Elizabeth I, recounted in horror how great multitudes of people—men, women and children, young and old—would vanish every May Eve into the greenwood to spend the night there and on their return, in addition to the branches of trees,

> . . . their cheerest jewel they bring from thence is their Maie pole, whiche thei bryng home with great veneration, as thus: thei have twentie or fourtie yoke of oxen, every oxe havying a sweete nosegaie of flowers placed on the tippe of his horns, and these oxen drawe home this Maie Poole (this stinckyng idoll rather), which is covered all over with flowers and hearbes, bound rounde about with stryn- ges, from the top to the bottom, and sometyme painted with variable colours, with twoo or three hundred men, women and children following it with greate devotion. And thus beyng reared up, with handkerchiefes and flagges streamyng on the toppe, thei straw the grounde aboute, bind green boughes about it, sett up sommer haules, bowers, and arbours hard by it. And then fall thei to banquet and feast, to leape and duance about it, as the heathen people did, at the dedication of their idolles, whereof this is a perfect patterne, or rather the thyng itself.*

What Stubbes in essence takes a long route around saying is that the Maypole was nothing but an enormous phallus.

Of all the plants that were held to be sacred to Pan, most special was the Orchis satyrion, whose bulbous root was used from time immemorial in potions for stirring up lust. Flagella- tion with supple green branches was also traditionally viewed as a great erotic stimulus bound up with the god's worship, and vestiges of this custom were preserved in European May Day

---

*Philip Stubbes, *Anatomie of Abuses* (London, 1583), fol. 94.

Figure 35

festivals where participants flailed at each other's legs with the boughs of young trees. At his most fundamental, the Emperor is simply a priapic progenitor.

At a more sophisticated level, however, he presents the embodied fatherhood or leadership of a nation or people. He is the will of heaven made manifest upon the earth.

The notion of a god-king is a fundamental one in human thinking. One can find many examples of it throughout history: Mesopotamia, Egypt, Greece, Etruria, Latium, China, Tibet, Peru, Japan; all at one time or another have made their male ruler into a god. It was a difficult idea to shake, moreover. "The Divine Right of Kings" persisted to the seventeenth century in England until Oliver Cromwell finally put a stop to it. But the

Continental emperors, deriving their very titles kaiser and czar from the line of Caesars, were mainstays of the tradition right up until the twentieth century.

The Emperor's meaning in divination is one of stability, potency, protection and realization, benevolent authority and paternal aid. Badly placed, he may indicate stubborn tyranny and the worst side of paternalism. But, generally speaking, like his consort he is a highly beneficent card, and his influence in a layout will always be an expansive, jovial one.

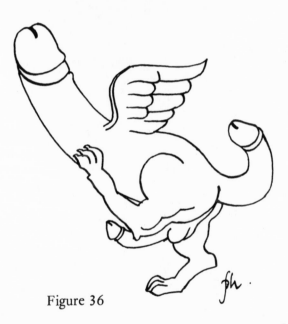

Figure 36

The Female Pope

Usually in modern tarot decks this lady appears as card two, after the Juggler. As the numbered sequence has crept in later, I have gathered together those cards which quite obviously are parts of a unit, if only a pair or more. The Female Pope or, as modern decks entitle her, the High Priestess, makes such a pair with the Pope, who in a similar manner has been retitled the Hierophant (see Figure 37).

So far we have examined those cards which represent Dionysus (the Fool), his tutor Hermes (the Juggler), and his earthly parents (the Empress and the Emperor).

With the Female Pope and the Pope we shall be casting our eyes up to heaven, or at least to the unseen world, and scrutinizing Dionysus' celestial parents, accounting for the divine part of the Mystery candidate's constitution.

In Jungian terminology, these two divine parents would probably represent the *anima* and *animus* of the individual. To the Romans they were known simply as a woman's "Juno" and a man's "Genius." On their birthdays, women would make sacrifice to their Juno and men to their Genius.

Juno—for this was the title of the Female Pope in old tarot decks, like the one painted for Filippo Maria Visconti in the fourteenth century—was the Roman name for the Greek goddess Hera, the heavenly sister-bride of Zeus, the All Father. She was the sister of Earth Mother Demeter (the Empress) and apparently her celestial alter ego.

The name "Hera" derives from a Greek word meaning "the mistress." She was always regarded as a stern goddess, as terrible in her wrath as her brother-consort Zeus. She sat beside him on a throne of gold whenever he presided at the councils of the gods. She was generally portrayed enthroned, robed and diademed with a high tiara from which a veil hung concealing

II

LA PAPESSE

Figure 37

her face. In one hand she would clasp a mystic pomegranate, in the other a staff surmounted by a cuckoo, for she held this bird in particular favor. In fact, some legends say Zeus only accomplished her seduction by assuming the shape of one.

In the English county of Sussex to this day a legend exists that each year spring is announced when the "Old Woman" lets the cuckoos out of her apron and speeds them on their way through the woods—possibly a belief stemming from Zeus' ruse.

In addition to being called Hera, she was also known by three other names: Pais ("Maiden"), Teleia ("Fulfilled") and Chera ("Solitary"). They show her to have been originally none other than the celestial symbol of femininity itself, the Moon. When her cult was transported to Italy, she became known as Iuno or Iana, which gave rise to two variants, Juno and Diana, both deriving from the same original root *div*, meaning "to shine." Not only was she worshiped as the queen of heaven from very early times with the surname "Regina," but she was regarded as special protector of the female sex, watching over all women from the moment of birth to that of death.

Hence the *anima* concept. She had very close links with Persephone, queen of the dead, as her sacred fruit the pomegranate shows. In fact, even as Demeter represents her earthly form, so does Persephone represent her dark aspect, or "Juno-Inferna," as she was also known.

Late syncretic paganism equated her with the Egyptian goddess Isis, whose cult had just arrived and been incorporated into Roman life. Though at first looked upon with imperial disfavor as something foreign and distinctly un-Roman, the cult of Isis rapidly gained adherents because of its solemn and imposing ritual and its assurance of life after death—a welcome relief to the decadent Roman life. In fact, it continued the tradition of Eleusis though, unlike the feminist cult of the Bona Dea, it was open to men and women alike.

After the advent of Christianity, the worship of a chaste goddess found expression in the cult of Mary, Queen of Heaven, and the attendant female saints that were one by one added to her retinue. Like the Sibylline Oracles and vestal virgins, chastity was a central theme in her worship. At Kildare in Ireland, Saint Bridget, originally Brigid, a Celtic queen of heaven, was portrayed as virgin abbess. In an illustrated manuscript dating from the fourteenth century,* the goddess in her planetary form as Luna is likewise shown as an abbess or nun.

But she was by no means always a pleasant figure. It was jealous Hera who was responsible for Dionysus' death. Closely associated with the goddess are those medieval legends concerning Morgan le Fay, King Arthur's witch-sister. She was also cast in the guise of a nun, and it was her jealous plots together with those of Modred, Arthur's bastard son, which finally encompassed the downfall of the Kingdom of Logres. Morgan le Fay, whose name derives from "Morrigan," a fierce Celtic goddess of death, represents the lady in her dark, inimical, underworld guise, who is ever seeking the ruin of her brother,

*MS. contained in Vatican Library, Rome, Catalog No. ms. Urb. Lat. 1398.

the resplendent solar King Arthur. A very similar tale of the queen of night's battle with the god of light, Zarastro, provides the basis for Mozart's occult opera *The Magic Flute*. Another medieval legend closely associated with this trump is the story of Pope Joan. It was first written down by the thirteenth-century French Dominican monk, Stephen of Bourbon, in his work *Seven Gifts Of the Holy Spirit*.

Joan—the name itself is an anglicized form of Juno—was said to have been born of English or German parents some time in the early ninth century. She was, according to the legend, educated in Cologne and during the course of her studies made the acquaintance of a Benedictine monk with whom she fell in love. Lest their guilty secret be found out, they fled to Athens, Greece, with Joan disguised as a fellow monk to allay suspicion. But their pecular idyll was not to last for long, for they were soon permanently separated by the death of Joan's lover. She then made her way to Rome, still in the guise of a man, and taking the name Joannes Anglicus (John of England) entered the priesthood! Such was Joan's piety that she quickly rose in the church's heirarchy, and it was not long before she had been awarded the red hat of a cardinal. But this ancient success story did not stop here. In the year 855 Pope Leo IV died, and "Cardinal Joannes" was so famous for wisdom and holiness that she quickly found herself elected to the office of pope.

The farce rapidly came to an end during the papal inauguration. Rotund Joannes in all his finery, to everyone's dismay, suddenly gave birth to a child on the steps of St. Peter's and promptly expired on the spot.

Reading between the lines of this grotesque story, we can perceive the very frayed remnants of the legend of the disguised goddess in her eternal quest for her dead lover. We can also relate it to the strand of ancient Greek tradition which tells of how Hera and Zeus spent their first three hundred years of matrimony in secret and that the only birth which resulted from it within this space of time was that of the unlucky Hephaestus, a premature one at that, accounting for the god of the forge's crippled condition.

During the fifteenth century, the Female Pope card still carried lingering memories of its ancient heritage. In a manuscript of the time dealing primarily with theology and its attitude toward gaming of all sorts, the list of cards in the section dealing with tarot has a marginal note beside the Female Pope, castigating those who deny the Christian faith, showing that ecclesiastical concern over votaries of the goddess was by no means extinct, even though the primary bugbear in heresy trials was the devil.*

In medieval and Renaissance talismanic magic, the nun image of Juno was used as a nota to invoke the power of memory itself. In medieval manuscripts she is often simply given the name Juno Memoria (see Figure 38). For in classical times the

Figure 38

*Sermones de Ludo cum Aliis (fifteenth-century illuminated manuscript in the collection of United States Playing Card Co., Cincinnati, Ohio), fol. 205-9.

type of magic most associated with Juno was the oracular function. The oracle, or sibyl, was a priestess who was skilled in the art of entering a trance and uttering prophecies while in it—the old shamanic technique. This trance was often brought on by gazing at a reflecting surface of some sort, such as a polished shield. The fortune-teller's crystal ball is its modern equivalent. The most primitive methods involved scrutinizing the depths of a lake or pond and letting the mind become bemused by the eddy of the water. Natural basins carved into the granite and fed by running streams, such as the Devil's Glen in Wicklow, Ireland, and the Swedish Blockula, were used for this purpose.

Pots of boiling water into which narcotic herbs were cast or even simply cups of clear water were also used. An example of the early use of such a divining bowl is given in the Bible: " . . . Is not this it [the silver cup] in which my lord [Joseph] drinketh, and whereby indeed he Divineth?"*

A similar method was used by Egyptian magicians during the nineteenth century. The ideal subjects were said to be either a prepubescent boy, a pregnant woman or a virgin maiden. The practitioner first inscribed in black ink the following diagram upon the left palm of the subject:

4	9	2
3	5	7
8	1	6

*Genesis 44:2-5.

This is the cabalistic Square of Saturn, a nota whose lines add up to fifteen whichever way you count. The seven magical squares, of which this is the first and simplest, have been used from very ancient times as planetary talismans. According to the *Key of Solomon*, the powers of Saturn can be used to acquire learning, although generally this dark planet governs more sinister operations.

The questioner next wrote the question he wished to ask the gods on a strip of thin paper and, together with a fistful of incense, burned it on the coals of a chafing dish.

He then poured a large blob of ink into the center of the square just under the 5 on the subject's outstretched hand and walked around him or her clockwise three times, posing the question out loud after each circumambulation. As the subject stared fixedly into the ink pool, he saw visions concerning the matter inquired about.

Another old method of receiving oracles which did not involve trance was by making use of bodily automatisms, such as twitching, sneezing or even rheumatic pains. These automatisms were often thought to herald certain events. " . . . By the pricking of my thumbs, Something evil this way comes . . . " is not such a quaint idea, it turns out. Experiments recently carried out have shown that a subject's blood pressure will often react to a psi impulse long before his conscious brain reacts, without the brain even registering it!* An ancient Greek method of using this awareness was to take an old ring, the older the better, and suspend it on the end of a long hair or piece of red thread. The free end was wound around the thumb or first finger in such a way as to be in contact with the pulse. The ring was then dangled in a bowl the edge of which had been marked with the letters of the alphabet. Questions were asked of it and it spelled out answers by striking the appropriate letters.

Another automatistic device, the "planchette," was invented

<hr>

*See E. D. Dean, "Plethysmograph Recordings as E.S.P. Responses," *International Journal of Neuropsychiatry*, Vol. 2 (October, 1966), pp. 439-46.

during the nineteenth century. It consisted of a small triangular or heart-shaped board supported by three small castors or wheels, or by two at the base, with a hole at the apex to hold a lead pencil. It was placed within a ring of letters or a sheet of plain paper, and the hands of the inquirer were laid gently on it. After a while it would begin to move, darting to and fro, spelling out or scribbling messages from the spirits of the dead. Unconscious muscular spasms on the part of the sitters were probably the cause. Prior to using it, however, the planchette had to receive a purification from hostile vibrations. This was accomplished by placing it for half an hour in the direct rays of the sun, its apex pointing south. It was then turned over repeatedly to absorb the full radiance and draw off the hostile vibrations. When not in use, the planchette had to be placed in the dark with its apex toward the north to preserve its neutrality and sensitivity.

The Female Pope's alternative title, High Priestess, is an eighteenth-century innovation and refers to her role as a Hierophantissa—the priestess who during the drama of the Greek Mysteries would enact the part of the goddess.

The card's appearance in a tarot spread is indicative of the great part played by someone's Juno in the situation, whether in sublimated form as deep feminine intuition or in frustrated underworld guise as hidden hostility and hypocrisy. She may be an actual person or merely a psychic construct, a dimly perceived though powerfully felt influence acting from beneath the threshold of consciousness.

Whereas the Empress trump illustrates the great goddess as the maternal mother of all living, active solely in a physical sense, the Female Pope shows her as immaculate Queen of Heaven, Sibyl or virgin nun—that is, physically inactive but psychically active in prayer and oracular intuition. In Freudian terms, the Female Pope may be related to the concept of the sublimated female libido, a willing renunciation of overt sexuality represented by the "queen of heaven" image or an unwilling one, sexual frustration, as the dark Morgan le Fay variant.

The Pope

In medieval representations of the classical gods, Jupiter, the Sky Father, is nearly always portrayed in the robes of a prelate or monk, often the pope himself. This is also how he appears in the tarot deck (see Figures 39 and 40).

Whereas the Female Pope represents Juno, the celestial stepmother of Dionysus, the Pope depicts his heavenly father, Jupiter, or, as the more ancient Greek civilization knew him, Zeus.

Zeus was the supreme god in the Greek pantheon, later equated by the Romans with their god Capitoline Jove. As the initiate of the Orphic Mysteries knew:

> . . . Zeus is the first, Zeus is the last,
> the god with the dazzling lightning.
> Zeus is the head, Zeus is the middle,
> of Zeus all things have their end . . . .*

His name, like those of Diana and Juno, also derives from the Aryan root *div*, "to shine," and it was the Greek words *Zeus Pitar*, Father Zeus, that gave rise to the Latin variant "Jupiter."

However, despite the Orphics' claim, Zeus was only one in a long line of supreme sky gods. Prior to his rule his Titan father, Kronos, had ruled the universe and before that his father's father, Ouranos. This divine genealogy was an attempt by mythographers to chart the influence of various sky cults which succeeded each other. Though they bore different names, the sky gods all had similar qualities. However, it was only with the advent of Zeus that the thunderbolt became singled out as the Greek Sky Father's exclusive symbol. As the supreme god, it was in Zeus' hands that the power lay of binding or absolving a man from his sins. Those guilty of great sacrilege turned to him for release from the Furies that pursued them as a consequence

*Otto Kern, ed., *Orphicorum fragmenta* (Berlin, 1922).

Figure 39

LE PAPE

T-shaped Hammer of Thor, the thunderbolt of the northern Zeus. It was frequently carved on Scandinavian runic inscrip- of their crimes. Inasmuch as Zeus could only be approached through his priests, it was to these that the guilty turned for absolution. This pagan idea passed into Christianity in the notion that the pope and his bishops, during the exercise of their offices, actually became the dispensers of divine blessing or approbation. As the old style Roman high priest had been *pontifex maximus*, the great bridgemaker or mediator between men and gods, so the new style pope became the vicar of Christ who held in his hands the "Keys of St. Peter," the ability to bless or curse, to bind or loose a man from his sins.

The traditional sign of benediction used by pagans and Christians alike has always been the sign of the cross. Far from originating with the instrument of Roman justice on which Jesus perished, the symbol derives from considerably older sources and recurs the world over as a solar or thunderbolt emblem. The swastika and the triskelion (three-pointed) rotating crosses are variants of this same "male" symbol, as was the

Figure 40

tions, like the sign of the cross later, marking the beginning and end of the message. Small amulets of the Hammer of Thor were also worn around the neck. Most important of all, it was frequently used as a holy sign of protection, traced with the fingers of the hand upon breast and brow, in exactly the same manner as the sign of the cross is used in the Catholic Church today. In fact, during the time of the conversion of the Saxons to Christianity, the sign of the cross was found to be so similar to the Hammer of Thor that many "converts" unwilling to totally relinquish their paganism resorted to its use with complete impunity. King Haakon the Good was reputed to have employed this device when blessing himself in the presence of his Christian bishop, or so his servant Sigurd related after the death of his master.

We can see the Hammer of Thor symbol still in use in the old Lincolnshire spell for curing the ague mentioned earlier. Three horseshoes, symbols of the triple-Moon goddess, were to be nailed to the foot of the afflicted person's bed, with the hammer being first laid crosswise on them and then used in the left hand to strike the nails in with the words: ,

> Father, Son and Holy Ghost,
> Nail the devil to the post!
> Thrice I strike with holy crook,
> One for God, and one for Wod and one for Lok!

The "holy crook" is the Hammer of Thor. It is also the crozier in the hand of the bishop or pope, used to strike on the door of a new cathedral during its consecration.

The fourteenth-century Visconti deck shows the Pope as Jupiter, while the Florentine Minchiate often represents him carrying a globe surmounted with a Jovian eagle. The most common pope representation in today's tarots is that shown in the Marseilles pack (Figure 39), a column-flanked figure wearing the triple papal tiara and grasping the triple patriarchal cross in his left hand. His right hand is raised in the act of benediction, first two fingers outstretched, the ring finger and little finger clasped by thumb to palm. At his feet kneel two cardinals.

To find the origin of this image we are going to have to dig around in an unholy spot, that old *grimoire* of planetary magic, the *Picatrix*. Here a talismanic image of Jupiter shows him crowned and enthroned with his hands raised above his head in priestly benediction. The throne itself is borne in the air at each corner by a winged figure, the prototypes for the later cardinals. This magical image, theoretically used for the acquiring of "riches, honor and felicity," itself dates back a very long way in its ancestry to Babylonian times, being what later came to be known by cabalists as the "Merkabah" throne, surrounded by the "Chaioth ha kadesh," four holy living creatures referred to by Ezekiel.*

With the amalgamation of Mediterranean paganism, Jupiter-Zeus came to be identified with the Egyptian gods Amen and Osiris, both chief deities of different cults. Whereas Amen was generally held to be supreme in Egypt between the twentieth and seventeenth centuries B.C., Osiris, whose cult flourished at first around the Nile Delta, held sway from the twenty-sixth

*Ezekiel:1-12.

Saitic dynasty, around 663 B.C., right up to the time of the Roman colonization in A.D. 30. Just prior to the closing of the Egyptian temples in A.D. 384, his cult was somewhat superseded by that of Sarapis, a combination of Osiris and the holy Apis-bull of Memphis, whom we encountered in Chapter 1.

In Sarapis the characteristics of Zeus-Jupiter, Egyptian Osiris and Greek Hades were fused together. Whereas the *sar* part of the name (from the Egyptian *asar*—Osiris) referred to his capacity as god of the underworld, the *apis* suffix (from the Egyptian *hapi*) showed the deity to be also a god of the earthly and celestial realms.

The cult of Sarapis was, like its twin, the Isis cult at first severely disapproved of by the Roman state, though eventually it established a firm footing in Italy as well as in Greece. Like Isis, Sarapis was worshiped especially as a deity of healing and fertility, and his temples were famous for the dream oracles which they offered to the public. His rites were particularly favored by the Ptolemy kings of Egypt and, like those of Isis, always retained their Egyptian flavor. In fact, Apuleius, the author of *The Golden Ass*, lets us know that in his day the cults of Isis and Sarapis were practiced side by side as an interlocking unit, as a celestial mother and father religion.

Thus the traditional import of the Pope tarot is a kindly one. Whereas the Emperor represents the mundane blessing of the father, the Pope indicates that the influence is more of a psychological and spiritual nature.

The alternative modern title for the trump, the Hierophant, indicates that he is a revealer of holy things, for that is what the word in the original Greek implies.

He is the priest that interprets the oracle's vision, the rationalization of the unconscious. Hence it is a card of inspiration or genius, the overshadowing demon or *animus* in a man, his link with the world of the gods. It may also represent an adviser of the querent's, one to whom he would turn in time of perplexity or spiritual quandary, possibly even a psychoanalyst, father-confessor or rabbi.

The Lovers

When we reach the Lovers in our tarot trump procession we leave the area of what are technically known as the lesser trumps, those cards which indicate the childhood of the young god, and move into the area representing his youth and manhood, the trials and pleasures offered by the world. In the lives of most savior figures such as Jesus, Buddha, Zoroaster, or Moses, there is nearly always a period when the future god-man, unaware of his divine mission, immerses himself in the ways of the world. The Lovers trump represents the first and most obvious pleasure of youth.

In classical mythology the power of love was chiefly embodied in two deities, often related together as mother and son: Venus and Cupid—or, as the ancient Greeks knew them, Aphrodite and Eros. Some stories claim that Eros became Aphrodite's constant companion and servant when she arose from the sea, for she was born from the foam of the waves that wash the shore of the island of Cyprus. Other tales, more generally accepted, maintain that the young winged god of love was the child of Aphrodite by Ares, the god of war. Some say he was fathered by Hermes, others by Hephaestus or even Zeus. Inasmuch as the Greeks knew Aphrodite by the name "Dione," itself a feminine form of "Zeus," meaning "goddess of the bright sky," she is quite obviously another aspect of the great goddess herself. She was also worshiped under the name Persephaessa, a variant of Persephone, and as "the far shining Moon" Pasiphaessa. She is undoubtedly the Queen of Heaven in amorous mood. Her winged son Eros also seems to have been worshiped as a double of Dionysus under the names of Palaemon, Taras and Melicertes.

Many tales were told of Aphrodite's numerous romances. There was hardly a god whom the lovely lady could not call husband at one time or another. But whereas Aphrodite was the patroness of all marriages and amorous liaisons, it was to Eros that the power of firing gods and mortals with love was attributed. He possessed a golden bow and a quiver full of arrows, some tipped with gold, others with lead. Those who were struck by the golden arrows promptly became infatuated with the first living object they set eyes on. But those pierced by the leaden tips fled in loathing from the first creature they encountered. Thus Eros played many cruel jokes and accordingly was treated with considerable deference by even the most powerful gods and goddesses, none of whom were safe from the jab of his barbs.

The usual method of getting Eros' aid in any amatory concern was through the wiles of his mother, Aphrodite. If she felt inclined, she would do her best through cajolement and bribery to persuade the perverse brat to accomplish the supplicant's desire. Stories of such comical deals were characteristic of the later legends of Eros, when he had become a figure of popular romance rather than awesome god. But the disciples of Orpheus preserved the true mystical significance of the young god in their teachings; he was the golden-winged son of the wind, firstborn of all the gods, hatched from the silver egg of ancient night, that great darkness whom witches later called Diana. As "Phanes," he revealed the light of day for, like the morning star, he heralded the morning. Plato supported and added to this myth through the mouth of his master, the philosopher Socrates.*

It was, however, as the willful and mischievous son of Venus that Eros passed into medieval lore. The Lovers trump depicts an Eros story, the Judgment of Paris, popular among medieval artists (Figure 41).

Paris, the second son of Priam, King of Troy, was destined from before birth to be the ruin of his nation. His mother had dreamed that she would give birth to a torch from whose flame the land would catch fire. Aesacus, the seer, recommended that

*Plato, *The Symposium.*

Figure 41

which was done. However, the child escaped death, being suckled by a wild boar, and was then brought up among shepherds. It was at this point that the gods lent a hand.

The goddess Eris (Discord) had, not unnaturally, been left uninvited to the wedding of the sea goddess Thetis and mortal Peleus. Piqued by such a breach of etiquette, this prototype of the child be left to perish on Mount Ida as soon as it was born, Carrabosse nonetheless arrived at the height of the festivities. Nonchalantly announcing that the gift she bore belonged to the fairest of them all, she tossed a golden apple into the assembly. After an undignified scramble, the apple fell to the clutches of three goddesses: Hera, queen of heaven, gray-eyed, chaste Athena, and beautiful Aphrodite. Each thought that the apple rightfully belonged to her. To settle the claim, Zeus ordered the three ladies to submit to the judgment of a mortal: none other than Paris, tending his flocks upon Mount Ida. Paris found it a difficult choice, especially as each of the goddesses waved various blandishments under his nose to sway his decision. "I shall make you king of Asia if you give me the apple," tempted celestial Hera. "I, on the other hand, will make you victorious in every battle you fight," countered Athena. Aphrodite merely unclasped her magic girdle and, with the aid of a timely golden arrow shot by Eros, who was hovering unseen above the assembly, won the golden prize without further ado. As a reward for the gift she promised the smitten Paris her constant favor and the hand of the fairest woman in the world. This turned out to be the Greek princess Helen, already wed to Spartan King Menelaus. Through the terrible war which resulted as retribution for Paris' abduction of Helen, the prophesied fate of Troy was sealed, and the city burned to the ground. In this terrible manner the slighted goddesses Hera and Athena were avenged. The usual medieval manner of depicting the Judgment of Paris was to show Paris confronted by either one, two or all three goddesses, while overhead Eros flutters unobtrusively, aiming his arrow at the man's heart.* Often, as in Florentine Minchiate decks, the Paris figure is shown kneeling while in Venus' outstretched hand an apple is sometimes indicated. Other tarots, such as the Visconti and Charles VI decks, simply depict a pair or pairs of lovers, but always overhead flies the all-important Eros. The legend also furnishes the additional meaning of the trump apart from simply "love"—namely, "choice" or "trial." Versions of this tableau frequently appear listed in collections of Venus images used for love magic in the Middle Ages. The *Picatrix*† mentions it first; the reputed wizard Peter d'Abano also uses it, and Heinrich Cornelius Agrippa mentions it in his second book of Occult Philosophy: " . . . A maiden with flowing hair wearing long white robes, holding in her right hand either a laurel branch, an apple or a bunch of flowers. . . . "

An image such as this, composed when the planet Venus was ascending in the first ten degree of Taurus, Pisces or Libra, was said to make men cheerful and to bestow beauty.

---

*A good pictorial example is Lucas Cranach's sixteenth-century "The Judgment of Paris," presently in the Karlsruhe Museum in Karlsruhe, Germany.

†*Picatrix Studies of the Warburg Institute,* Vol. 27, trans. into German by H. Ritter and M. Plessner (London, University of London, 1962).

On the other hand, a Venus image made with Venus ascending in Taurus gave the love of woman " . . . the figure of a naked maid, with long flowing hair, bearing a looking glass in her hand and a chain bound about her neck—Near her is a handsome young man holding the end of the chain in his left hand, and with his right hand caressing her hair. Above them flies a little winged boy carrying an arrow . . . "

Both of these images are combined in the Lovers trump. The chain bound about Venus' neck may be a version of her traditional magical girdle in necklace form, like that of the northern Freyja. For Freyja was considered to be identical with Venus, as we can see when we examine the name of the fifth day of the week: "Friday" comes from *Freyas daeg*, and in Italian, *venerdi* is Venus' day.

The mysterious-looking glass in the goddess' hand is another interesting indication of this fusion of cults; it is actually a medieval interpretation of the sacred rattle of Egypt, the sistrum, which Isis—or her other forms, Hathor and Bast—often carried in their hands. It symbolized divine merriment and rejoicing.

Thus the type of witchery indicated by the Lovers is that delicately referred to as the ability " . . . to make those who are ugly beautiful . . . "*

Apart from covering the field of cosmetics and perfumes, this definition included the vast realm of love charms and aphrodisiacs. Perfumes and love potions frequently poached on each others' territory: whatever smelled good and made one more attractive if one wore it was undoubtedly venereal in essence, and therefore highly suitable for compounding love spells. For instance, an aphrodisiac unguent for anointing the erogenous zones would be considered magical if composed of powdered frankincense, powdered myrrh and powdered camphor, all mixed with a small quantity of rose water and a few drops of musk and left to macerate for two days in the direct heat of the sun.

*C. G. Leland, *Aradia, or the Gospel of the Witches* (London, David Nutt, 1899), p. 15.

The rose was considered a flower particularly sacred to Venus, as was the myrtle. Both of these plants often figure in love potions for this reason, as in this Portuguese philter dating from the eighteenth century containing 1 pint rosewater, 1 pint orange flower water, ½ pint myrtle water, 2/3 spirit of musk, 2/3 spirit of ambergris.

Ambergris, the favorite scent of Madame du Barry and an exotic ingredient of many modern perfumes, is produced from an intestinal secretion of a cachalot or sperm whale. Apart from its sweet odor, the very fact that it is produced by a marine creature lent a venereal quality to it for, as we have seen, Venus was originally a marine goddess, born of Cyprian sea foam. Marine products of various sorts often appear in love potions

Figure 42

for this reason. Cleopatra dissolved pearls in wine, an old Oriental trick; Roman Apuleius recommended spiced oysters, cuttlefish or lobsters for those who would be ardent in their passions. Coral especially was considered to be under the rule of Venus.

Anything which tasted sweet was also naturally linked immediately with the power of attraction. Hence honey, and later sugar, rated high on the list of love-potion ingredients in various combinations: honey and ginger; honey, pine nuts and almonds; sugar, rosewater and almonds . . .

Apples, not unnaturally, also played a large part in love spells. So did camel's milk at one time, for, according to Agrippa, the camel was another of the beasts held sacred to Venus by the ancients.

Magical talismans inscribed with pictures like the Lovers trump were also used to promote love for the bearer. Sometimes these were accompanied by traditional Venus sigils and symbols such as those engraved on the copper bracelets known as armillaries of Venus. Pictorial Venus images may still be seen on old talismans, such as John Dee's "Tuba Veneris" ("Horn of Venus"). This is a parchment illustrated with a picture of the goddess bearing a cornucopia, the horn of plenty, at present in the keeping of the Warburg Institute in London.

That formidable witch, Catherine de Médicis, wife of Henry II of France and in all probability the prototype for Snow White's stepmother, also possessed a secret talisman engraved with both Venus sigils and the naked figure of the goddess bearing the golden apple (Figure 42).

And, like Snow White's stepmother, in addition to relying on sorcery, many witches would reinforce their spells with drugs. One of the drugs used in love spells was the Marquise de Pompadour's trusty standby, tincture of cantharides. This noxious ingredient known more generally by its less romantic title of spanish fly is an irritant produced from the beetle Cantharsis vesicatoria. The active chemical cantharidin is derived from it, which is fatal if taken internally. It is amazing that King Louis XV lived through his mistress' administrations. Ignorant and wholesale applications of such drugs helped to earn witches the unenviable title of *veneficae*, "poisoners," very early in history as much as did any deliberate poisoning.

Whenever you come across the Lovers in your tarot layout you will know that either the light of the goddess Venus has fallen upon the querent's life or upon that of someone close to him. Or he may be confronted by an emotional choice of some sort, either his own or one which has to be made by someone he is involved with.

The Chariot

"Of all the gods who live on Olympus thou art the most odious to me, for thou enjoyest nothing but strife, war and battles! Thou hast the obstinate and unmanageable disposition of thy mother Hera, whom I can scarcely control with my words!" So speaks Zeus to his son Ares, god of war, in Homer's *Iliad*. It was a generally held sentiment.

Ares, or Mars, as the Romans knew him, was not particularly popular among the other Olympian gods. He was stern, humorless and brutish, a monolithic war machine. Undeniably he had a certain sex appeal; his illicit romance with Venus speaks for this. They were finally caught in bed together by Vulcan, Venus' cuckolded husband, who by way of revenge put them on display, trapped in their inelegant position by means of a fine bronze net. The goddess Eris, whom we met in the last section, was a constant companion of Mars on the battlefield, as were his two henchmen Phobos (Fright) and Deimos (Panic). The two satellite moons of the planet Mars were appropriately named after them when they were discovered by Asaph Hall in 1877.

Although, strictly speaking, Mars was the son of Jupiter, the syncretists considered him to be yet another aspect of the All Father himself.

Whereas the throne shown in the Pope's trump shows divine stability, the Chariot shows the deity mobilized for destruction. The lore surrounding the mysterious "Merkabah" throne of the medieval cabalists reflects this notion, for this Holy Seat of the Father was a chariot as well.

In India the early warrior-caste sky deity Indra rode a fiery chariot and wielded thunderbolt weapons; so did the popular Vedic sky god Rudra, from whom in turn evolved the post-Vedic Siva. Vishnu, in his eighth incarnation as Jagganatha, lord of the world, also rode a mighty chariot which received his name "juggernaut." The Scandinavians worshiped the sky god of battles as Thor or Thunor the Thunderer, while the Irish Celts knew him as Balor of the Terrible Eye.

Figure 43

The Evil Eye itself is often used in myth as an alternative to the thunderbolt as the war god's weapon of destruction. We find it occurring in stories of the Egyptian lion-headed goddess Sekhmet, the personification of the Sun's destructive power. She is often portrayed as simply a winged disc, the terrible Eye of Ra. Charged with a mission of destruction against mankind by her master Ra, the Eye went on a rampage of such ferocity that, unable to stop the creature he had unleashed, Ra caused the fields of Egypt to be swamped with a mixture of beer and pomegranate juice. Thirsty Sekhmet, mistaking the potion for human blood, fell into a drunken stupor, and thus the human race was saved at the eleventh hour.

The ancient Greek story of Phaëthon, son of the Sun, ties in closely with this legend. Phaëthon at one time may have been the name for the planet Venus, which later came to be known as Phosphorus the Morning Star. His parents were, according to some legends, Eos, the dawn goddess, and Helios, the old Titanic Sun god who ruled before the advent of Apollo. According to others his mother was Clymene, another name for Persephone. When we see from Hesiod that Aphrodite became enamored of the young Phaëthon and sought to raise him to the rank of an immortal god, we perceive that we are again being confronted by the same old Mediterranean legend of the great goddess and her lover-son in yet another guise. Phaëthon was the brother of Circe and Aeëtes and the uncle of Medea. According to Ovid, he begged his father, Helios, to let him drive his solar chariot across the sky unaided.* In his inexpert hands the terrible steeds of the Sun eluded his control, and the blazing chariot plunged in a wild arc toward earth, setting fire to all directly beneath. Zeus, seeing that earth was in imminent peril of destruction, launched a bolt of lightning at the runaway

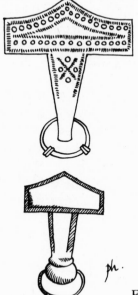

Figure 44

*Ovid, *Metamorphoses*, Ch. I, v. 751.

chariot and struck the youngster in midflight. His body, burning like a torch, plunged like the Wormwood Star into the waters of the river Eridanus.

In medieval paintings and illustrations Mars was frequently depicted standing in his chariot, sometimes brandishing a whip,* a halberd† or simply a sword.** Sometimes the steeds that drew the chariot were winged, as in the chapel of the Palazzo Publico in Siena. The Mantegna deck of the fifteenth century shows Mars standing in the chariot fiercely brandishing a sword. In this instance the chariot has a canopy but no horses drawing it. The earlier Charles VI deck of 1392, however, depicts the war god carrying a battle-ax, which, like the Hammer of Thor, was a more ancient representative of the thunderbolt than the sword (Figures 43 and 44).

The chariot symbol itself is one which occurs frequently in the lore of talismans. According to Abano and Agrippa, martial notae should portray the armed and crowned god wearing a sword and carrying a long lance in his right hand. He should, of course, be mounted in a chariot. The time to construct this talisman was when the planet Mars ascended in the first ten degrees of Scorpio, the sign which it rules or is most powerful in. A talisman like this was said to fill a man with courage and provide great opportunities for success in wars or competitions.

Closely associated with such martial sorcery were magical methods of securing vengeance, such as the following taken from Florentine witchlore: Cast powdered cumin and incense on hot coals, stirring them around vigorously with a sharp knife point. Fumigate each room of the house with the smoke, chanting as you do: "I do not stab the incense, but rather the body, soul and all the feelings of the wretched person who has sent ill-fortune to my house!"

*See *Ovid Moralisé* (1480 text in Colart Mansion, Bourges, or ms. Thott 399, Konegelige Bibliothek, Copenhagen and ms fr. 143, Bibliothèque Nationale, Paris. (See bibliography for additional date.)

†See illustrated manuscript, Catalog No. ms. fr. 6986, Bibliothèque Nationale, Paris, for an example of this.

**See relief by Agostino di Duccio in the Tempio Malatestiano, Rimini, Italy.

Having done this, take a yellow slip of paper and two steel nails wired together in the form of a cross (the Hammer of Thor) and place both paper and cross in the red-hot coals. Then, if you don't know who your enemy is, throw the coal, ashes and cross into a running stream or river; if you do know who it is, bury them under the eves of his roof. This was thought to secure complete transmission of the spell!

In herbal magic, all plants of a hot and acrid nature were said to be governed by Mars. Euphorbium, an acrid red resin exuded by plants of the spurge family, as inflammable as it is poisonous, was a prime ingredient in many martial charms. The traditional incense of Mars was composed of euphorbium, bdellium, black and white hellebore root, gum ammoniac, powdered lodestone and sulphur, mixed with the blood of a man, a black cat and the brain of a young deer!

However, any plant of a hot or prickly nature was deemed equally powerful from a magical point of view: holly, stinging nettles, ginger, even common kitchen pepper. It was the idea rather than any chemical value in the plant itself that counted.

The Chariot trump shows the initiate-god, Phaëton, riding forth in power. War was the second mundane trial for all young men in the ancient world, as it still is in many parts of the modern—first love, then military service. In the sacred procession of the Dionysian triumphs, love and severity walk hand-in-hand, Venus and Mars, the lover and the warrior. When you see the Chariot in your tarot layout, you will know that a struggle is indicated in the cards. A strong indication of a victory is given if it is well placed with harmonious cards or, alternatively, the possibility of defeat, withdrawal or sustained injuries if reversed or badly juxtaposed.

Justice

The Fool has been initiated into the mysteries of love and war, symbolized by the planets Venus (the Lovers) and Mars (the Chariot). He has been educated by Mercury (the Juggler), knows that he is a royal child of the earth (the Empress and the Emperor) and also that the other side of his nature is divine (the Female Pope, Juno, and the Pope, Jupiter. He has one more planetary lesson to learn: the burden of time, symbolized by that card now known as the Hermit, but once simply called the Old Man. He also has the four major moral lessons to learn known by medieval scholars as the cardinal virtues: justice, temperance, fortitude and prudence.

According to Christian theologians, the cardinal virtues are the four which occur naturally in humanity without the intervention of God. Three more, the so-called theological virtues, were considered to emanate solely from God: faith, hope and charity. They were added to the list later, making seven virtues in all. The absence of these seven virtues in a man gave rise to their corollaries, the seven mortal sins, deadly because they were theoretically the root causes of all other sins. These were vainglory, or pride, covetousness, lust, envy, gluttony, anger and sloth.

Both the seven virtues and the seven sins were frequently portrayed in medieval morality plays, often in dramas like *Everyman* which demonstrated the fortunes and misfortunes of a central human figure caught between the opposing armies of heaven and hell.

The four cardinal virtues did not originate with Christianity, however. Christian moralists like Ambrose, Augustine and Thomas Aquinas built them into their theological schemes, but the virtues themselves go back all the way to Aristotle and Plato, possibly to Socrates. From the Greek philosophers they passed to Rome, where they became an integral part of Latin memory training systems. The great orator Cicero, writing in the first century B.C., makes considerable use of them as four great cornerstones of virtue, which he defines in a manner typical of Stoic philosophy as a "mental habit harmonious with reason and the natural order of things."* But they were not simply abstract qualities. Back in the fourth century B.C., Aristotle, Plato's disciple, tried to explain the formation of the physical world by drawing upon ideas current in the East and formulating them into the doctrine of the four elements.

This stated that the physical world consisted of primordial matter which lay in a twilight state of potential existence until it was impressed by form. The four ways in which this form manifested were called the four elements, which, according to Aristotle, were only to be distinguished from one another by their properties.

The names of the elements were fire, whose properties were dryness and heat; air, with the properties heat and fluidity; water, with the properties fluidity and coldness; and earth, with the properties coldness and dryness. The elements blended into one another by means of their shared properties: fire into air by heat; air into water by fluidity, etc. (see Figure 46). In fact, according to this theory, one element could be changed into another by simply combining it with its opposite and making use of two of its qualities—the coldness from water combined with the dryness of fire will produce earth. Because everything in the world was composed of a combination of these elements, this theory left the way open for the ingenuity of later alchemists to try to turn useless matter into useful—generally, lead into gold.

In the tarot deck, the doctrines of the cardinal virtues and the four Aristotelian elements seem to be combined in the symbolism of the Minor Arcana suit emblems—Rods, Swords, Cups and Coins—as well as the virtue trumps. In the oldest tarots Fortitude (Strength) clasps a column or brandishes a

*Cicero, *De inventione,* trans. by H. M. Hubbell (Loeb Classical Library), II, l. iii, 160.

Figure 45

scepter, club or branch in the air. Justice, on the other hand, grasps the sword. Temperance pours liquid from one vessel to another, an obviously aquatic symbol. While Prudence, now called the Wheel of Fortune, shows foolish Midas bound by the golden chains of his own avarice to the round of earthly suffering. The virtue trumps seem to be moral lessons typical of the Stoic element in Orphism, which have to be learned by the Fool before he confronts his supreme ordeal.

This first virtue card in modern packs is Justice (see Figure 45). The figure portrayed on the card is always female. The legends behind it are those of a group of goddesses closely connected with the wisdom of Jupiter-Zeus.

Themis, whose name in Greek means "a natural law," was the daughter of Gaia, the first Earth Mother, and Ouranos, the original Sky Father. She was a Titan, in fact. Young Zeus took her to wife, according to the poet Pindar, showing her to be a version of Hera. From their union were born the Horae, deities whose names mean "the right time," whence our word "hour." Their duties were to bring all things to fruition. Also born to

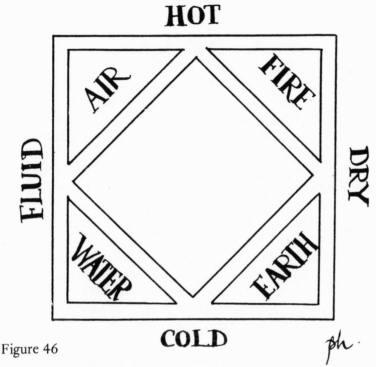

Figure 46

Themis and Zeus was a daughter, Astraea. She was said to have lived on earth during the Golden Age, that time before the Flood when men lived peacefully together in an earthly paradise. As the wickedness among men increased, she withdrew from the world and finally made her abode in the heavens, where she is now known as the zodiacal constellation Virgo.

During the Renaissance the traditional figure of justice with sword and scales was claimed to be Astraea's* but it might just as well have been that of Themis, her mother.

Paralleling the story of Astraea's birth is that of the other wise goddess, Athena. Metis, her mother, whose name means "wise counsel," was, like Themis, a Titan, being the daughter of the early sea deities Oceanus and Tethys. She also mated with Zeus, who, following the advice of his grandparents Ouranos

*See Filelfo, *Canzone Morale* (Florence, 1431).

and Gaia and the example of his exiled father Kronos, swallowed her whole before she had a chance to give birth! The reason he did this unlikely thing was to forestall the threat that any offspring of his by all-wise Metis might pose him.

Athena—for such was the name of the unborn child—was not to be thwarted, however. Hephaestus, others say the Titan Prometheus, struck Zeus' head with a double-edged ax and Athena, fully grown and clothed in golden armor, leaped from the wound to take her place among the other Olympians.

Athena wielded her father's all-destroying thunderbolt and was worshiped both as the deity of dispassionate justice and as the mistress of wars. She was in constant conflict with Ares, whose battle tactics she despised, being those of brute strength. Hers were those of skill and dexterity. Though, as her name "Parthenos" shows, she remained a virgin, she patronized various heroes at different times. The Romans worshiped Athena under the name Minerva, which appears to derive from the root *mens* or *manas* meaning "the mind." The owl was traditionally the bird sacred to her because of its reputed vigilance. In fact, owls and wisdom have remained symbolically linked in Western folktales down the ages.

The school of justice is where one learns how to resolve a problem impartially, how to weigh the matter carefully in the scales of wisdom before applying the sword of retribution. When the Justice trump appears within a spread it counsels "think and weigh the situation impartially." It is a card of balance and equilibrium, often implying the natural order of things as expressed in the Eastern concept of dharma. However, it may also represent a person, not necessarily a judge but an arbitrator or referee known to the querent with whom he is now or will soon be involved.

When upside down or ill-placed it indicates the reverse of all these things: bias, prejudice; partiality and inequality; or a corrupt and unfair arbitrator. For Justice, like her prototypes Athena and Themis, though she holds the divine fires of retribution in her hand, must always remain upright and balanced, else she is not just.

Fortitude

In contemporary tarot decks Fortitude, or Strength as it is also known, is usually presented as trump number eleven, falling between the Wheel of Fortune and the Hanged Man. The fifteenth-century manuscript *Sermones de Ludo** on the other hand, lists it as trump number nine, between the Chariot and the Wheel of Fortune. Similarly the manuscript places Justice at the end of the line between the Judgment (Resurrection) and the World, as opposed to its present-day position between the Chariot and the Hermit, as card number eight.

Florentine Minchiate decks do otherwise. Often they simply gather the four cardinal virtues together between the Lovers, which figures as trump number five, and the Chariot, trump ten. Temperance first, Fortitude second, followed by Justice and, finally, the Wheel. Apparently the order in which the moral lessons were learned did not particularly matter.

I shall adopt the Minchiate's procedure and gather the cardinal four together. This will enable me to deal with them at the same time, for they interrelate considerably.

Fortitude in modern packs portrays a woman either wrenching open or forcing shut the gaping jaws of a lion (see Figure 47). This is the conventional medieval representation of that virtue. The figure may be that of the nymph Cyrene, a devotee of the chaste Moon goddess, Artemis. The Sun god, Apollo, saw the girl wrestling unarmed with a lion one day and, taking a fancy to her, spirited her off in his chariot to North Africa after speedily consulting the wise centaur Chiron on the advisability of the match.

The result of his union with her was Aristaeus, a mysterious huntsman-god who was compared for his strength and wisdom

---

*Op. cit. *Sermones de Ludo cum Aliis* (fifteenth-century illuminated manuscript in the collection of United States Playing Card Co., Cincinnati, Ohio), fol. 205-9.

with both his father, Apollo, and his grandfather, Zeus, by his worshipers. He himself married Autonoë (Dionysus' aunt) and fathered Actaeon upon her.

Actaeon, like his father, was brought up to be skilled in all the arts of hunting by the centaur Chiron, who seems to have

Figure 47

played a continuing role as the family tutor. While hunting the wildwoods with his pack of fifty dogs, Actaeon accidentally came across the goddess Artemis herself bathing in a woodland stream. According to one version of the story, the wild hunts-man attempted to rape the goddess, who, enraged, turned him into a stag, an animal sacred to her. Whereupon Actaeon's dogs fell upon their master and tore him to bits. Some tales say that Actaeon was not really transformed but only assumed a stag skin and antlers. But all agree on his ultimate fate.

In ancient Aricia, now known as l'Ariccia, in Italy, the worship of Artemis and her wild lover survived the fall of Greece in the shape of the cult of Diana Nemorensis—Diana of the Woods. Actaeon became the Rex Nemorensis, King of the

Woods, whose priest regularly perished in combat at the hands of a successor, always a runaway slave, who then assumed his office as consort of the goddess.

The mythical genealogy of Actaeon's family may well be a symbolic account of what later became this Diana Nemorensis cult. Its priests and priestesses were regarded as sons of the god and daughters of the goddess respectively. Instead of dealing with a love chase enacted by Zeus and Demeter or Hades and Persephone, the primary actors were now the Sun and the Moon, in the forms of Apollo and Cyrene, then Aristaeus and Autonoë, and lastly Actaeon and Artemis. It is obviously a version of the Diana and Lucifer story of the Florentine witch cult.

There are alternative Fortitude figures to that of Cyrene, however. One of these, occurring in the 1392 Charles VI deck, shows a figure breaking a Corinthian column in two. Though the tarot figure has become a female one, the prototype was probably male, being none other than the Biblical strong man Samson breaking the pillar to which he was bound after being betrayed by his faithless Delilah. The Bembo deck, on the other hand, shows a club-wielding man about to take a swing at a fearsome lion which crouches at his feet. It is the Greek hero Heracles, or as the Latins knew him, Hercules. The Nemean lion, which crouches at his feet, is, like the seven-headed Hydra and the chimera, just one of the terrifying creatures he encountered during his famous labors imposed by Hera. And, like the hounds of Actaeon, the monsters sent to devour Dionysus, the serpent of Delphi and even Lucifer's pussycat, they are all manifestations of the great goddess. For Hercules, like Samson, Jason and Actaeon, is also a solar hero, a son of the Sun, battling with the older goddess cult, even as he is finally destined to wed one of its representatives—the oldest way to reconciliation. The Stoics saw great occult importance in these legends of Hercules over and above their historical significance. Gnostic sects like those of the magian Marcos certainly carried on the tradition.

Some of the stories of Hercules may well have passed into European legend in the form of the exploits of the *commedia dell'arte* character Pulcinella, who later was to become the cruel character of children's puppet shows, Punch. Both Hercules and Pulcinella kill their wives, the former in a fit of madness engineered by Hera and the latter out of sheer rage at her nagging tongue; both wield a large stick; both cheat death; both get caught up with exploits concerning a dog, a regular common or garden sort in Mr. Punch's case, the infernal Cerberus in Hercules'. And, lastly, both end up victorious over the devil— Old Nick in Mr. Punch's expoits, Hades in those of Hercules.

In fact, the stories of Hercules and Pulcinella themselves closely parallel the exploits of the tarot Fool. This is certainly no accident. We are undoubtedly dealing with a version of the same legend, as can be seen when one compares the lives and miracles of Hercules and Dionysus from childhood onward, the serpents, Hera's jealousy, and so on.

Fortitude represents the trials of strength of the Fool. It also contains the idea of a man struggling with his primitive instincts. Seen as a virtue, this has been interpreted by some as a transformation or sublimation of sexuality. According to medieval occult lore, the practice of chastity brought with it magical powers. One of these was thought to be an ability to control wild beasts. The legend of the unicorn bears testimony to this. The only person who could catch a specimen of these mythical single-horned horses was said to be a chaste, beautiful maiden. Only if she were truly a virgin would the unicorn gently approach her and willingly allow itself to be led into captivity.

In old alchemical prints the symbolism of the lion and the unicorn occurs fairly frequently. Whereas the lion symbolized the aggressive, fiery force of the Sun, the unicorn, or sometimes the deer as a variant, represented the fleeting lunar element. That the lion should figure so frequently in the design of Fortitude is obviously no accident.

This power of taming beasts has always been seen as magical to some degree. Often it was preserved in the form of a secret which was handed down within families. Both witch and gypsy were credited with knowledge of it. It is closely connected with the concept of animal totemism—a mystical bond between man and beast. This bond, traditionally shared by the witch with her animal familiar, seems to be identical in effect with that existing between beasts and members of societies like the Horse Whisperers in Ireland and Horseman's Word in Scotland. Con Sullivan, a famous eighteenth-century Horse Whisperer, either could not or would not explain the secret of his power over horses, just as Cunning Murrell, the twentieth-century wizard of Hadleigh, was unable or unwilling to explain the source of his power over cattle and small animals.*

The secret appears to be one shared by Indian tribes of North and South America and gypsies of Hungary and Middle Europe alike, and it lies at the root of such fairy-tale elements as helpful animals who are coerced into friendship by sharing the hero's food. This, in fact, is how the bond is always maintained, the food often being doctored with herbs.

One herbal nostrum consisted of a cake of oatmeal, honey and purple medick (Medicago sativa). This had to be carried next to the skin to absorb the perspiration of the trainer, who would then feed it to the horse after it had been without food for twenty-four hours. The subtle bond between man and beast was maintained through the trainer's saliva: he spat into the horse's mouth when the time came to groom it. However, saliva and perspiration were not the only substances by which the link was made. The trainer's burnt hair introduced into the animal's food would suffice, or even a drop of his blood—a method shared by the witch in making a psychic link with her animal familiar.

Figures like that shown on Fortitude were used as talismans for binding men and beasts. One is mentioned by Agrippa. It was to be made when Mars was ascending in the second face of Aries, between the tenth and twentieth degree, and it used a version of the Fortitude image, a man astride a lion, carrying an upright bared sword in his right hand, in his left the head of a

*See Eric Maple, *The Dark World of Witches* (London, Robert Hale Ltd., 1962).

man. Another was the ever-popular icon of Saint George and the Dragon or, alternatively, Saint Michael and the Dragon. Both derive from similar mythological roots.

An even more exact description of the Fortitude trump is listed by Agrippa under his account of solar images as a rod-carrying king astride a lion, large of body and limb. What better description of Hercules?

When the card turns up in your tarot layout, it counsels "stand fast," "firm resolve" and "take courage." On the other hand, when it is reversed it can betoken stubborn folly, obstinacy, and a certain fool rushing in where angels fear to tread.

Temperance

We have already seen that the four virtue trumps have alchemical overtones consonant with their elemental symbolism. Temperance equates with the element water. The trump usually portrays a woman pouring liquid from one container into another. In modern decks she is winged like an angel (see Figure 48). The design is a classical medieval image of the virtue temperance which, according to the dictionary, means "moderation" or "self-restraint." It is the third Stoic lesson that the Fool must learn.

Various theories have been advanced as to who the mysterious figure pouring the water actually is; maybe it was originally Ganymede, a young Trojan prince who was abducted by Zeus to become the cup-bearer of the gods and whose task it became to refill Zeus' cup with the nectar of immortality when it was empty.

Or it could be identified with the eleventh sign of the zodiac, Aquarius, the water carrier. In fact, the Egyptian zodiac of Dendera shows Aquarius carrying *two* containers, and he was identified by the Egyptians with Hapi, the god of the Nile, whose waters were the source of life both agricultural and spiritual for their land. Again we see the same idea appearing: fruitfulness and inspiration.

The second-century Gnostic Marcos may also have some relevance here as he did in the previous trump. Marcos taught a brand of Valentinian Christianity which embraced a number of pagan doctrines, including a complex scheme of divine emanations similar to the one used by the cabala. Like that doctrine, he also relied heavily on a Pythagorean system of numerology. What distinguished Marcos' brand of Christianity from other Gnostic cults was that he celebrated the Eucharist using two chalices instead of one. By pouring the contents of one into the other, he mixed water with the wine, the water being equated in his scheme with Sophia, "divine wisdom," which had fallen to earth and been whirled about in the dark empty spaces, and the wine with the fiery spirit of the Savior Christ. This was compared to the descent of a bridegroom to a bride, who would in his embrace save her from the prison of matter and reascend with her once more to the heavenly spaces. The double-cup water-into-wine Eucharist of Marcos was viewed by his detractors as simply a sleight-of-hand trick parodying the legend of Jesus; in fact, it may well have been drawn originally from the rites of Dionysus as the god of wine. *Aradia, or the Gospel of Witches* (Leland) records it under the list of witchy abilities granted by Diana simply as the power to change water into wine. Lead into gold would have been an equally good symbol. In the ornate language of alchemists, the water was "the gluten of the eagle," the wine "the blood of the lion," both of which

Figure 48

were mingled in a "philosophical egg," or curcubite—the gourd-shaped lower portion of an alembic (still)—and then subjected to the heat of the athanor (furnace).

From the time of the great eighth-century Arab alchemist Jabir ibn-Hayyan onward, the key to the alchemist's dream was thought to lie in a mysterious mystic utterance attributed to Hermes himself and said to have been first discovered engraved on a tablet of emerald. It obviously derives from Gnosticism, and it reproduces in mystical terms the idea propounded by Marcos, namely the redemption of matter by means of divine fire:

> Truly it is without lie, accurate and most certain, to say that what is above is like what is below, and what is below mirrors what is above, so that wonders can be worked by means of this Cosmic Unity. All things become real by reason of this Unity, and everything was originally created by adaptation from it.
>
> Its father is the Sun and its mother the Moon. The Wind carries it in its womb, and the Earth nurses it.
>
> It is the author of every miraculous work in the entire universe.
>
> Its power is total.
>
> It may be brought down to Earth, where it proceeds to separate the Earth element from the Fire element, the spiritual from the gross. Then gently and with great ingenuity it rises from Earth to Heaven again.
>
> Only to descend one last time having united in itself the occult Powers from above and below.
>
> In this same manner you may come to possess an illumination of the entire Universe, such that all obscurity will fly from you. This Thing is the essence of power, for it embraces everything subtle, and penetrates everything solid.
>
> In this manner our world was made. And in this manner may many marvelous things be accomplished.
>
> And because of this I am named Hermes Trismegistos [thrice great] because I hold three parts of the wisdom of the entire world.
>
> What I have to say concerning the "Operation of the Sun" is now finished.*

*"Hermes Trismegistus," author's translation, date uncertain. Text available in J. F. Ruska, *Tabula Smaragdina* (Heidelberg, 1926).

This mysterious "Operation of the Sun" so frantically sought after by the alchemists was the production of the "philosopher's stone," a legendary substance which when added to a crucible of molten lead would produce shining gold, or even more miraculously, if taken internally by human beings would cure all ills and prolong life indefinitely—the "elixir of life." It was also known as the quintessence, the fifth element, the one from which the four Aristotelian elements were supposed to have been originally derived and into which all four could be turned by skillful manipulation.

Theoretically, by using this quintessence as what we today would call a catalyst, "immature" metals such as lead could have their evolutions speeded up and turned into "mature" metals such as silver or, ultimately, gold.

In view of our present-day viewpoint of atomic science, it is curious how close the alchemists were to truth. Transpose your scale of values from a medieval one where gold was accounted the most precious metal to a modern one where a high-yield radioactive isotope would top the list, and the philosopher's stone, alias the quintessence, looks remarkably like atomic radiation, that ubiquitous phenomenon atomic physicists deal with every day in their laboratories. Taking into account Albert Einstein's revolutionary equation of mass and energy, on the one hand, and the artificially induced evolution of such metals as plutonium into uranium by radiation, on the other, were the alchemists so wrong in essence? Many of the alchemical riddles reveal new and provocatively intriguing depths when viewed in the light of modern particle physics rather than eighteenth-century Newtonian science.

But as C. G. Jung first noted,* most alchemical tracts can be read from a purely psychological point of view as well as a chemical one; the quaint symbols are here seen to refer to psychic conditions and processes rather than scientific events. In view of their Gnostic origin, this was probably the original intention.

*See C. G. Jung, *Psychology and Alchemy*, trans. by R. F. C. Hull (London, Routledge and Kegan Paul, 1963).

When Temperance appears in the tarot spread it is said to bring with it a sense of consolidation, unifaction and resolution. This may mean the temporary stalemate of two conflicting forces prior to achieving a synthesis. Thus it may be a card of concession. Or, less abstractly, it may represent a third person who acts as arbitrator, like an escrow agent who holds in safe keeping the securities of both parties, representing both their interests and acting as a medium of exchange during a transaction. It necessitates concessions toward a common goal. On the other hand, if the card is reversed, it may augur an ill-advised partnership marred by clashing interests.

The Wheel of Fortune

This card represents the last moral rest that the Fool has to pass before he embarks on his great ordeal (see Figure 49).

According to ancient Greek myth, a man's destiny was ruled over by three strange goddesses known as the Moirae or the Fates. "Fate" is also a word which means a fairy or enchantress, as in Morgan le Fay's Latinized name, Fata Morgana. Strictly speaking, however, the word *moira* means "portion," and according to Orphic traditions the three portions are those three faces of the Moon herself: new, full and dark. Thus we are confronted by the triple goddess again as virgin, mother and hag.

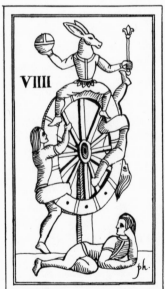

Figure 49

But that is not all. The Moirae were also spinners. They spun the thread of a man's destiny, and so powerful was their dictate that even Zeus had to obey them. They were his superiors, for their worship was a Titanic one long preceding that of the Olympian. The Romans came to know the three sisters as the Parcae and the Scandinavians spoke of them as the Norns. In all instances they were thought of as mysterious spinners, and it was probably here that the spinning wheel acquired its witchy associations as a machine of fate, as in the story of the Sleeping Beauty.

The Saxons came to know the three Norns as the three Wyrds or singly as the goddess Wyrd. Shakespeare modeled his Weird Sisters after them, those three witches who prophesied Macbeth's success and final doom.

However, the triple goddess did not always labor alone in her distiny-spinning. According to *Aradia*,* she spun the lives of men while Lucifer gallantly turned the wheel. Lucifer may be identified partially with Janus, who was the Roman two-headed god of doorways. His name furnishes us with the month January, and his image provided one of the chief Gothic images for the virtue prudence. His gaze was thought to encompass both sides of the doorway, past and future, and according to the witches of Florence, it was to him that a man had to pray for luck:

> Jano is a spirit with two heads, one of a Christian [i.e., human] and one of an animal, and yet he hah a good heart, especially that of the animal, and whoever desires a favor from them should invoke both, and to do this he must take two cards of a tarocco [tarot] pack, generally The Wheel of Fortune and the *Diavolo indiavolato* [the Devil] and put them on the iron [frame] of the bed and say:
>
> > *Diavalo che sei capo*
> > *Di tutti i diavoli!*
> > *La testa ti voglio stiaccare*
> > *Fino che o spirito di Jano*
> > *Per me non vai a pregare!*
> >
> > *["Thou devil who are chief*
> > *of all the devils!"]*

*C. G. Leland, *Aradia, or the Gospel of the Witches* (London, David Nutt, 1899), p. 19.

I intend to crush thy head
Unless the spirit of Jano
Does not pray for me!"]

As we shall see later, the two-headed Janus figure also provides part of the inspiration for the Devil trump.

In early tarot decks, four figures are often shown bound to the Wheel of Fortune. They all have asses' ears and the top one wears a crown. Each utters a Latin motto translating as "I will rule," "I rule," "I have ruled" and "I am without rule." They are pictures of the Fool himself, in this instance portrayed in the guise of King Midas. After barely escaping with his life as a consequence of opting for the fatal gift of turning everything he touched to gold, this foolish king of antiquity again underscored his stupidity by giving the judgment to Pan in a musical contest between the goat-god and Apollo. Apollo rewarded him with asses' ears for his choice.

The notion of a man's body actually being tied to the spinning wheel of fate may originally derive from the Greek legend of Ixion. Medieval art portrayed the devil spinning damned souls on a fiery torture wheel fairly frequently.† Ixion was a king of the Lapithae, a race usually thought of as half brothers to the centaurs, with whom they were in a constant state of conflict. They were thought to have been the original inhabitants of Thessaly, a Mediterranean island which in Lucius Apuleius' time was notorious for its witches and sorcerers.

Ixion's wife Dia was probably an archaic form of the great goddess herself, for the name comes from the same root as Juno and Diana. Ixion was highly favored by Zeus at first. Consequently he resided in Olympus with the gods, where he fell in love with the goddess Hera. Zeus suspected an illicit love affair between Ixion and his wife and substituted an image of her made from clouds, upon which the enamored Ixion begat a

---

*C. G. Leland, *Etruscan Magic and Occult Remedies* (New York, University Books, 1963), p. 130.

†For an example of the devil portrayed thus, see the medieval illuminated manuscript in the Bodleian Library, Oxford, England, catalog number ms. Douce 134, f.83.

son, half horse and half man—the first centaur. Furious at this revelation of perfidy, Zeus thereupon bound the unlucky Ixion to a fiery wheel to spin for all eternity.

In some Wheels of Fortune, Fortuna, the Italic version of Wyrd, is portrayed either seated precariously in the center* or bowling it merrily along the ground like a circus performer on a unicycle.

In modern packs the transformation of the initiate into a beast prior to sacrifice (for this is originally what the Midas-Ixion symbol implied) has itself been transformed into something else.

Instead of portraying the ass-eared fool with his Latin utterances signifying "I will rule," "I rule," "I have ruled" and "I am without rule," many of the modern decks, taking their cue from the Marseilles pack, show three strange-looking creatures riding the wheel. One of them is an ape or doglike animal usually thought to represent the composite Egyptian god Hermanubis. Another is a horse or wolf-headed man, said to be Typhon, the Egyptian Saturn. The third is a man-headed lion, the Sphinx.

The relevance of these symbols actually comes from medieval scholasticism, where in addition to being portrayed as Janus, Prudence also was depicted as a *three*-headed figure whose triple image signified past, present and future. The left-hand head of a wolf or old man stood for the power of *memoria*—memory, the past. The central head of a mature man or a lion signified *intelligentia*—intelligence and the present. The right-hand head of a youth or dog symbolized *providentia*—foresight and the future.† The idea that Prudence consisted of these three elements goes back even further. The great Platonist orator Cicero, writing during the first century B.C., states categorically that "Prudence consists of the knowledge of what is good, what is

---

*See the Bembo tarot pack.

†For an example of this image, see Titian's "Prudentia," Francis Howard Collection, London.

bad, and what is neither good nor bad. Its parts are Memory, Intelligence and Foresight . . . "*

In fact, Macrobius, a pagan syncretist writing in the fourth century A.D.† claims that the origin of this Prudence image was the three-headed infernal hound Cerberus. An example of this image may be seen at the Castel Gandolfo, in Italy.

When simply shown as a seated figure, Prudence frequently held a circle in her hands, a symbol of time. Which brings us back once again to the wheel symbol.

We have followed the progress of the initiate from babyhood through mundane schooling to where he is caught up in the revolution of fate's spinning wheel. Like Midas, he is advised to "be prudent." Like Lucius, Marsyas and Actaeon, he has been changed into an animal by his desires. He has reached the nadir of the wheel's revolution—the devil's gold has changed to dust. He is experiencing the tyranny of the senses and the transience of fortune. He has earned his asses' ears.

---

*Cicero, *De inventione*, Ch. II, v. 53, 160.

† Macrobius, *Saturnalia*, French translation with text by H. Bornecque and F. Richard (Paris, 1937), Bk. I, ch. 20.

The Hermit

Modern tarot commentators have conjectured that this trump represents anything from the "light of the world" or the "ancient of days" to any one of the many mythical sages encountered in occult literature, such as Solomon, Hermes Trismegistus, Christian Rosenkreutz and Apollonius of Tyana. Its true identity is quite different and can be discovered easily enough if one takes the trouble to examine early decks.

The Hermit or, as it used to be called in Italian decks, *il Gobbo* (the Old Man) represents Saturn, the last of the astrological planets encountered by the Fool other than the Sun and the Moon. (See Figure 50.)

Saturn became identified with the idea of old age and time through the confusion of his Greek name Kronos with the Latin

Figure 50

god Chronus, meaning "time." Saturn was the bringer of old age, but he was also the giver of longevity, as we shall see when we study the legends surrounding him.

According to the ancient Greeks, Kronos, or Saturn as the Latins subsequently knew him, was one of the Titan sons of the first Sky Father and Earth Mother, Ouranos and Gaia. Father Ouranos, far from being a model father, loathed his offspring to such an extent that he thrust them back into the Earth the instant she gave birth to them. Poor Gaia, burdened by this cruel imposition, plotted among her children to slay their tyrannical father and produced an iron sickle for the purpose. One night as the Sky approached the Earth to cover her, Kronos took the sickle and castrated Ouranos. He then seized power in his stead.

Far from learning by his father's mistakes, Kronus became as much of a tyrant as Ouranos had been in his time. Having been told by his mother, Gaia, that he, like his father, would live to be supplanted by a powerful son, Kronos swallowed his children as soon as his wife, Rhea, gave birth to them. This is simply a borrowed version of the earlier Ouranos-cult legend. Rhea, an earth goddess like Gaia before her, was also instrumental in plotting her husband's downfall with the aid of her children, led by young Zeus. She saved him from Kronos by presenting a stone wrapped in baby clothes to swallow in place of the child. Zeus subsequently wrested power from Kronos and banished him to rule the Isles of the Blessed.

Thus Kronos-Saturn came to be looked upon by the ancients as representative of tyrannous old age and oppression. As Father Time, he was often portrayed carrying the sickle or scythe provided by his mother, Gaia. The planetary symbol of Saturn still depicts this reaping hook.

The astrological influence of Saturn has always been considered to be a malign, oppressive one, and has earned it the title of "the Greater Infortune" (as opposed to the Lesser, which was Mars).

In astrological charts it often presages gloom and doom generally but more specifically a heavy, cold, dark and oppressive sort. The notion of Saturn swallowing his children has been linked to that sobering one of "Time bearing all his sons away," although most modern astrologers like to think that he is not all bad. From starting life as a Greek sky-god, he ended up in Italy as an agricultural deity, for the name "Saturnus" probably derives from the root *sator*, which means someone who sows seed. The symbolism of the sickle or scythe and the fall of the fertilizing blood of Ouranos obviously ties in here. Hence there is a curious earthy quality about Saturn which turns up in various medieval magical texts. For instance, *The Greater Key of Solomon* states that the days and hours of Saturn are good for causing good or ill to "Business, possessions, goods, seeds, fruits and similar things . . . " Also, strangely enough, " . . . to acquire learning . . . ," for Kronos was renowned for his cunning.* This is the interpretation modern astrologers favor most; he is the archetypal schoolmaster, stern on the surface, maybe, but benevolent underneath.

One classical tale claims that after the Old Man was deposed by Zeus, he fled to Italy and became the first Golden Age king. Possibly the word *latuit*, meaning "he hid," gave the land its title "Latium." Indeed, Saturn himself was said to be hidden in some mysterious manner beneath the stones of the Capitol in Rome.

It was from Saturn that the name of the midwinter festival Saturnalia derives, as does Saturday, the seventh day of the week, the day of repose and finality. Both carry the same idea: the completion of a time cycle followed by a rest period. The Old Man is in retirement.

According to Francis Barrett, who took his magic from the pages of Abano and Agrippa, a talisman showing a Saturn image, such as a graybeard cloaked in black leaning on a staff and bearing a sickle, constructed on a Saturday at the hour of Saturn, with Saturn ascending in Capricorn, brought to the bearer all the benevolent powers of the planet.†

*The Greater Key of Solomon, trans. by S. M. Mathers (Chicago, de Laurence Scott, 1914), pp. 10-11.

†Francis Barrett, The Magus (New York, University Books, 1967), Pt. II, Chap. XXXVI, p. 160.

In medieval art Saturn is frequently depicted thus, bearing an hourglass and leaning heavily on a staff or hobbling on two crutches. Alternatively, he is sometimes shown as a man with the head of a stag or ass, like Actaeon or Lucius. In fact, his trump has very close connections with the Wheel of Fortune, for Saturn himself was sometimes referred to as Prudence.* One might say that in the same way that the Lovers appears to be balanced by Temperance and the Chariot by Justice, so is the Old Man by the Wheel of Fortune.

Some Italian decks, like the Florentine Minchiate, have separated the stag symbol from that of Saturn as an animal lurking in the background of the card. For the stag itself was also associated with longevity, so much so that stag antler occurs frequently in many old recipes for the so-called elixir of life.

Another longevity potion ingredient associated with Saturn was the herb sage, at one time considered remarkable for its supposed life-prolonging virtues. The variety of wormwood known as southernwood or old man is also special to Saturn, as is myrrh, that ancient embalming gum whose bitter smell can be detected in the incenses of most high Anglican and Roman Catholic churches. "Myrrh is mine, its bitter perfume breathes a life of gathering doom . . . " says the old carol.

Other more unusual examples of Hermit tarots show Father Time appropriately surrounded by the symbols of the four elements and the twelve signs of the zodiac. The Mantegna deck actually calls him Cronico, in Neoplatonic philosophy the genius of time and the cosmic principle of chronology. However, in modern packs though his staff or crutch remains the same, the hourglass of time has changed into a lantern. Any hint of the stag seems to have vanished completely.

During the Dark and Middle Ages another curious body of magical lore came to be associated with the power of Saturn: the lore of brazen heads. These mysterious objects were thought to have been possessed by a number of suspected necromancers,

---

*As by the fourteenth-century Franciscan John Ridewall, in *Fulgentius Metaforalis*, reprinted in *Studien der Bibliothek Warburg*, IV, Leipzig, Berlin, 1926).

including a pope! The idea of such artificial androids goes back a long way. In classical myth the wizard-smith Daedalus is said to have constructed one, a brazen giant, Talos, whose task it was to patrol the shores of the island of Crete and defend them from marauders. The monster was all but invincible, though his fall was ultimately engineered through the magic of Medea.* Vergilius the Sorcerer, a character loosely based on a Dark Age-eye view of the Roman poet Virgil, whose miraculous exploits play a major part in the tales of the Gesta Romanorum, was also credited with the construction of a brazen android for similar peace-keeping purposes. However, it was the French Pope Sylvester II, known before his elevation to the papacy as Gerbert, possibly one of the greatest scholars of the tenth century, who according to legend was the first to build an oracular bronze head. According to William of Malmesbury, the brazen head promptly predicted Pope Sylvester's death in Jerusalem. Hardly surprisingly, His Holiness declined to visit the Holy Land during his term of office, but to no avail. The prediction came true. He died while celebrating mass in the Jerusalem Church in Rome. According to legend, Sylvester had sold his soul to the devil, and after his death his tomb became a center of supernatural activity, shedding tears whenever a pope was about to die! Gerbert's spectacular rise to the papacy must have seemed supernatural to his contemporaries, but it was probably due more to the favor of a onetime pupil of his who subsequently became the Holy Roman Emperor Otto III than to the attentions of Old Nick. During his lifetime Gerbert accumulated an enormous library of classical authors, totally ignoring those of the church fathers. Which leads one to suspect that maybe there is more to the legend of his heretical interests than meets the eye. Certainly he was well acquainted with the sciences of Islam, for during his lectures he used both the Arabic method of counting on an abacus with a cipher-counter to represent tens and astrolabes to illustrate the positions of the heavenly bodies.

*See Apollonius of Rhodes, The Voyage of Argo, trans. by E. V. Rieu (London, Penguin Books, 1959).

Roger Bacon was another head-building scholar who was not only whispered about but actually persecuted for his supposed sorcery. According to one old story, this thirteenth-century alchemist, credited by some with the discovery of gunpowder, decided, like Daedalus, to surround his homeland with a wall of brass as a means of defense against its enemies. For added security he built a brazen head which when animated could be consulted on matters of state. He and Friar Bungay, his companion in the black arts, thereupon set about conjuring up a spirit in a deserted wood to ask it how to animate the head. The spirit instructed them to fumigate the head with rare spices for a month, at the end of which time it would give utterance. However, if the first words were not heard and responded to, the experiment would come to naught. Bacon ill-advisedly left his dim-witted servant Miles in charge of his laboratory when the head decided to speak. It began its oracular ministry with the words "Time is!" When this message went unheeded, the head improved upon it a few minutes later with the words "Time was!" Five minutes later, still finding Miles totally oblivious to the importance of the occasion, the head signed off with: "Time is past!" and exploded into fragments.

An identical story is also told of Albertus Magnus, with the ecclesiastic Thomas Aquinas, the "angelic doctor," cast in the role of Miles. Instead of being a simpleton who causes the head's destruction by an act of omission, Aquinas deliberately smashes the automaton in a fit of rage, incensed by its constant chatter during his attempts to study.

Many of the tales told of Bacon, Gerbert and Albertus Magnus appear to be interchangeable. The story of the enchanted garden of Albertus Magnus recounted in an earlier chapter is also told of Bacon. Inasmuch as Gerbert was credited with the invention of the clock as well as the introduction of astrolabe and abacus, the brazen head would appear on the surface to be an amalgamation of all these things in a single poetic image.

However, the notion of "time is, was and is past" has a distinctly chronological Saturnian ring to it, recalling the Wheel of Fortune motto of "I will rule, I rule, I have ruled and I am without rule." The brazen head was not simply a misty medieval inkling of a computer. In fact, the nineteenth-century wizard Francis Barrett gives specific instructions on how to make one, and they are decidedly occult:

> ... They [the ancients] made ... from the operations of Saturn, and also Mercury, an image of cast metal, like a beautiful man, which, they said, would foretell things to come; and made it on the day of Mercury [Wednesday] on the third hour of Saturn (5 P.M.), the sign of Gemini ascending, being the house of Mercury, signifying prophets; Saturn and Mercury being in conjunction in Aquarius, in the ninth house of heaven [that of Philosophy among other things].
> . . .
> Moreover, let Saturn have a trine aspect in the ascendant, and the Moon in like manner, and the Sun have an aspect on the place of conjunction; Venus obtaining some angle, may be powerful and occidental; let Mars be combust [within a degree or two] by the sun, but let it not have an aspect on Saturn and Mercury; for they said that the splendor of the power of these stars was diffused upon this image, and it did speak with men, and declare those things which are profitable for them.*

One would have thought that anyone clever enough to carry out those instructions would have little need of the brazen head.

The Hermit trump is said to presage a Saturnine influence, slowing things down and occasioning deliberation when it appears in your layout. If well aspected, the slowdown will be a beneficial one, a time for prudent planning and clever manipulation. Reversed or in an inappropriate position, it may turn out to be an unnecessary and irksome delay caused by unreasonable caution, fear, stubbornness, oppression or even deceit, for all of these are Saturnine qualities of a less desirable sort.

---

*See Francis Barrett, *The Magus* (New York, University Books, 1967), Pt. II, Chap. XXXVI, p. 160.

The Hanged Man

Dionysus, the ass-eared Fool, has reached the end of his Saturnalia. His time has elapsed. He must perish in order to be reborn as Iacchus, even as the seed must descend into the earth to grow again the next year.

In Greece, images of Dionysus were frequently hung in trees as a means of securing fertility for the vines and crops.* This ancient belief persisted in Europe under the guise of such practices as stoning an effigy at Lent known as a Jack o' Lent. "Jack" may possibly be derived from "Iacchus" or "Jacco." After the effigy had been taunted and abused, simulating the Titans' treatment of Dionysus, it was frequently burned, shot at or simply thrown down a chimney. The Saxons, however, continued to hang it from a tree.

Figure 51

Though he was known as Jack o'Lent, some thought the effigy to be that of Judas Iscariot. Actually it symbolized the entire spirit of the winter carnival over which the Lord of Misrule had presided. The bound, hanging figure shown in the Hanged Man is undoubtedly this Judas Iscariot (see Figure 51). The coins sometimes shown pouring from the twin pouches he clutches in either hand are the thirty pieces of silver for which he sold Jesus to the Romans. He has been "baffled"—hung by his heels, the ancient punishment inflicted upon debtors. But lurking behind this orthodox image is that of Jack o'Lent, and behind that is Dionysus embarking upon his descent into the underworld.

The myth of the dying god is a shamanic one, as we have already seen. The Hanged Man shows us the death itself.

An ancient Nordic poem, "The Lay of the High One," on the surface seems to refer to the crucifixion of Jesus, but actually it deals with the exploits of Odin who, as we saw earlier, was not only a frosty version of Greek Hermes but an archsorcerer also, a prototype shaman.

> For all of nine stormy nights
> I hung upon the tree,
> Wounded by my own blade
> Odin consecrated to Odin
> An offering to myself,
> Bound to that Mighty Tree
> Whose roots men know not!
> > None gave me to eat
> > None gave me to drink
> > Down into the abyss I wandered
> > And sought out the Runes!
> > Then I fell into darkness with a great cry!
> Rebirth I attained
> And also wisdom
> For I grew strong and exalted in my growing.
> Thus from one Rune was I led to a second,
> From one act to another.

In view of what we know of shamanic initiation rites, the Hanged Man trump appears through its symbolism to hint strongly at this sort of initiation ordeal, probably of a self-imposed nature.

The Far East, in a characteristically less violent exposition than Western stories of Odin or Jesus, has the Buddha begin his spiritual conquest of death and illusion seated at the foot of the archetypal bodhi tree rather than suspended from it. He is bound to it by his own vow rather than physical bonds. The more primitive shaman, however, following the ancient practice of shackling the limbs of corpses before burial in case they decided to return to pester the living, would bind his actual limbs before entering a magical trance. This practice appears to carry over into present-day ritual initiation processes. Freemasons use a "cable tow" to bind the candidate hand and foot prior to his induction.

The order of the Golden Dawn, itself partially drawn from German Rosicrucian sources,* by all accounts practiced a rite which employed binding and hanging upon a cross in its first initiation to adept-hood, the "adeptus minor" grade, and in its annually performed "Corpus Christi Ritual." In both the chief participant was bound to a "cross of suffering." In the first instance this was a prelude to illumination, in the second a means of absolution for the order's corporate annual "karmic debt"!†

Some occultists insist that there is a practical as well as symbolic purpose to this bondage,** on which recent researches into sensory deprivation may have begun to cast light.

Theoretically, the first step onto the astral plane can be made by binding the limbs, covering eyes and ears and suspending the entire body in such a way as to induce a feeling of free-floating. Instead of being filled by the usual sense-derived data, the

---

*See A. E. Waite, Shadows of Life and Thought (London, Selwyn & Blount, 1938) and Israel Regardie, My Rosicrucian Adventure (Chicago, Aries Press, 1936).

† Israel Regardie, The Golden Dawn, Vol. II (Chicago, Aries Press, 1938), pp. 211-12, 274-75.

**See J. A. Vernon, Inside the Black Room (New York, Clarkson N. Potter, Inc., 1963).

consciousness of the subject will be filled with mental data in the form of hallucinations and fantasies. Whereas the yogi or Buddhist enters this twilight state easily enough through his constant practice of mental introspection, the shaman relies on actually removing the stimuli which normally occupy the central position in his consciousness, in this way subjecting himself to the phantasmagoria of the unconscious mind into which he enters as a protagonist in a drama. It is an antique version of Muldoon's "incapacitation" technique.

By all accounts the dream state encountered is a surrealist one, resembling the imagery of painters like Hieronymus Bosch, Pieter Brueghel and Salvador Dali. Everyday objects in outlandish proportion, miniature or outsize, appear side by side with bizarre hybrid forms, animal, vegetable or mineral. The most characteristic feature of this state, however, is that everything is in a constant state of motion—changing from one shape into another, flowing together to form one where two had been, or simply moving from one place to another. It is this constant astral flux and metamorphosis which constitutes part of the "Maya" illusion of the Buddhist and Vedanta mystic.

Just as the physical body was immobilized in order to better pay attention to this astral realm, so must this constantly shifting world be tamed, penetrated, seen through by the mystic before further progress toward enlightenment can take place. As we saw on preceding pages, when he reaches this astral level, the forms which confront the mystic spring from an area of consciousness which appears partly his own and also partly alien. Thus he will be imposing order upon wild animals of his unconscious which are his and yet not his, both objective *and* subjective, projected before his eyes like demons which he must encounter and tame.

This was also undoubtedly true for the Orphic initiate. The lessons learned under the headings of the various planets and virtue tarot trumps now played their part. The resilience they had imparted to the initiate gave him the ability to confront the shape-shifting specters before his inward eye without qualm, even to tame and bind them.

In Greek mythology this ancient shape-shifting entity encountered by the initiate is sometimes pictured under the guise of a primordial sea-god, the Old Man of the Sea. Actually there were originally three mysterious brothers who each held this title: the Titans Nereus, Proteus and Phorcys. All of them were expert shape-shifters. The wandering hero Menelaus captured the mysterious Proteus and bound him tightly, though the god changed shape repeatedly from lion to serpent to leopard to pig to a stretch of water and, finally, to a tree in order to evade capture. These ruses failing him, Proteus finally told Menelaus the answer to his problem, the exact course for his ship to reach home safely.

A comparable story is told of Hercules and Nereus, who successively changed from lion into stag into serpent to evade capture. A similar progression was undergone by Dionysus before he met his death at the hands of the Titans.

Whether the Fool is being slain as a benefactor whose royal blood is demanded to sacrificially regenerate the fertility of the crops or whether, like Odin, he is offering himself to himself in the pursuit of occult wisdom is all one. The idea of exchanging the mundane for the spiritual is the central one.

And this is the fortune-teller's meaning for the Hanged Man trump. Jack o'Lent is both paying the price for his worldly folly and making his entry into the twilight realm. In a divination his import is one of wisdom, often an occult, intuitive variety, attained through sacrifice. Alternatively he may represent constriction of some sort, usually psychological.

Badly placed or reversed he may represent either an ill-conceived sacrifice or simply a loosening of strictures. Like the Fool and the World, he is an extremely important card in the tarot deck. In Jungian terms, he represents the turning point in the psychic life of the individual and the coming to grips with the unconscious. It is the means whereby the descent into the underworld is made.

Death

This is perhaps the card most likely to scare any novice consulting the tarots; but according to modern interpretations, the Death trump, like the planet Saturn in astrology, is really not at all as bad as it seems on the surface. With considerable juggling modern decks have also managed to keep it in the supposedly unlucky thirteenth place in the trump series, although often the grim title "Death" is tactfully omitted, leaving people to draw their own conclusions about the skeletal reaper.

In most tarot decks, Death is depicted as a skeleton carrying in his hands a scythe before whose sweep fall prelates, princes and all. No one is excepted. (See Figure 52.)

Figure 52

As we have just seen, the scythe or reaping hook is a symbol of the god Saturn and, indeed, Death is one of the grim

Figure 53

medieval faces of this deity. "Time" has become "mortality" (see Figure 53). From the word "mortality" itself we can trace back an even more ancient lineage for him. Mors, or Moros as the Greeks knew him, was one of the children of black, primordial Night. In fact, he is a masculine version of the three Moirae, those Weird Sisters whose exploits we examined a few pages back. Thus Moros was in effect destiny himself, supreme above all gods, whose will not even mighty Zeus could gainsay. Like the triadic Fates, he also possessed two other aspects, Thanatos and Ker. In Greek vase paintings Thanatos is usually portrayed as a benevolent, dark-winged genius, often attending upon a sleeper with his brother Hypnos, Sleep. The poet Euripides, however, described him in more terrible guise, as black-robed and striding among men with a drawn sword. Such a description would perhaps be more appropriate to the third brother, Ker. He himself was closely linked with three female deities, the Keres, who, robed in blood and fire, accompanied

Ares upon the battlefield spiriting off the souls of the dead. They were in fact southern versions of the Nordic Valkyries, those female "choosers of the slain," and were thought to be synonymous with the Moirae themselves. Thus we come full circle.

Both northern and southern versions of these death goddesses were known as the Hounds of Hell, and they frequently took the shape of monstrous hunting dogs whose barks rang out through the darkness when they hunted men's souls. In Greece they were also known as the Erinyes, or Furies, black goddesses with gorgon heads who dogged the steps of those guilty of sacrilegious crimes. This canine death symbolism also appears in the dog Cerberus, whose image gave rise to the three animal figures on the Wheel of Fortune and whose task it was to guard the gate of the underworld from intruders.

Classical mythology contributed a further facet to the medieval Death hybrid in the figure of Charon, an old ferryman whose task it was to ferry the souls of the departed across the Acheron, one of the many rivers which bounded the underworld. Corpses were usually buried with a coin between their lips as a bribe for truculent Charon, for if the poor soul appeared at the crossing without his "obolus," Charon would deny it passage. It would then be destined to spend the rest of eternity wandering the dreary meadows of asphodel bordering the Acheron as an unlaid ghost.

Charon persisted well into the Renaissance. Dante made use of him in his themes, and he crept into a sickbed vision of the great sculptor Benvenuto Cellini:

> I was utterly weak and exhausted, hardly able to draw in my breath, but my mind remained as clear and agile as it had been before I was ill. All the same, one day a terrifying old man appeared at my bedside and tried to drag me off by force into his enormous boat. . . .
>
> Lodovico asked me to describe what it was I thought I saw, and what he was like. But while I was sketching him in words, the old man seized me by the arm and tugged me forcibly towards him. At once I screamed that they must rush to my help, because he was going

to throw me down into his loathsome boat; then, as soon as I uttered the last word, I fell back senseless, imagining that I had in fact been hurled into the boat. . . *

According to Orphic initiates, when the candidate for initiation made his underworld descent, the golden bough was the one talisman which would force Charon to ferry him into the presence of the gods of death and back again. This golden bough may be a reference to the shamanic rod or some type of hallucinatory herb used to help bring on the visions. The majority of such hallucinatory agents also fell under the heading of poisons. Depending on the dosage, most of them could be used for either illumination or death.

Undoubtedly herbs of this kind provided the basis for legendary transformation potions like Circe's and those mentioned in *The Arabian Nights* and *The Golden Ass.* English and Continental witches appear to have preserved these traditions in the various prescriptions for their "flying ointments." In light of contemporary hip-talk, this quaint term is not without a certain humor.

Many of these prescriptions are still in existence in the works of Johann Wier and other demonologists. Here are four for comparison:

R$_X$ 1. Aconite, parsley, poplar leaves, soot, deadly nightshade, water parsnip, cinquefoil, sweet flag, bat's blood, oil.

R$_X$ 2. Water parsnip, aconite, deadly nightshade, cinquefoil, lard, soot.

R$_X$ 3. Water parsnip, smallage, cinquefoil, lard, soot.

R$_X$ 4. Bat's blood taken at the full moon, cinquefoil, poplar leaves, soot.

Deadly nightshade appears in two of them. Various drugs are derived from it in modern pharmacopoeia, including belladonna. The water parsnip was a well-known medieval soporific used for allaying fevers. Aconite was a particularly deadly poison, used for baiting wolf traps. Cinquefoil, or five-finger

*The Autobiography of Benvenuto Cellini, trans. by George Bull (London, Folio Society, 1966).

grass as it is called today, was a witch herb par excellence on account of its pentacle-shaped leaf.

Other well-known hallucinatory witch herbs were datura, "the devil's apple," and its close cousin mandrake. Datura is used to this day by American shamans for inducing initiatory hallucinations.*

In Egyptian myth, the boat of the dead was manned by the jackal-god of embalming, Anubis. During the syncretic period he was looked on as a manifestation of Hermes, for he also functioned as an intermediary between gods and men and guided souls safely to and from the underworld. In the Roman Isis cult, however, the goddess herself ferried the mysterious boat, as she also did in ancient Celtic myth. The coracle of Ceridwen seems to have filtered into Arthurian romance as the bark of Morgan le Fay.

In Christian times, the role of psychopomp passed to an angel, the feared Angel of Death or, as the cabalists knew him, Azrael, the Dark Angel of the Doors. He was very similar in concept to the Greek Thanatos.

All of these legends no doubt contributed to Death's image. But the trump symbol of the skeleton is more than simply an antique image of death. In view of the possible shamanic origins of the tarot deck, the contemporary fortune-tellers' sweetened interpretation of the trump as "change" or "transformation" would seem to have more truth to it than it possibly deserves. For one of the most common features in shamanic initiation throughout the world is that the candidate for initiation experiences the frightening illusory reduction of his body to a skeleton. All flesh is magically consumed off him, by being boiled off in the caldron, burned off by fire or simply torn off by wrathful spirits. This is, of course, what the Orphics considered the terrible death of Dionysus implied. In old alchemical terms, before the philosophical gold could be created, complete putrefaction had to be experienced.

*See Carlos Castaneda, *The Teachings of Don Juan* (Berkeley, University of California Press, 1968).

If Death appears in a tarot spread, the consultant's immediate reaction will probably be one of panic, especially if he knows nothing of the tarot. It can, indeed, mean just that—if not the actual event of death, then maybe someone's preoccupation with it. On the other hand, it can mean change; not an idle change, but a purgative, deep-seated one whereby the ego is stripped bare of old values preparatory to reinvestment with new—brainwashing, if you like. Whereas the Hanged Man has taken the first step toward illumination, binding himself spiritually and morally to the achievement of his goal, Death strips him bare of all pretensions prior to leading him into the presence of the underworld deities.

The Devil

Having been purged of all worldly identification by his struggle with the ministers of death, the candidate for shamanic power now enters the presence of the king of terrors himself.

The figure of the Devil, usually numbered fifteen in modern tarot decks, is like the other tarot archetypes, the end result of a long line of traditions which have been fused into a single succinct image. In order to penetrate deeper into the identity of Old Nick than the customary Christian bogeyman interpretation, we must remember the axiom that the gods of a dead religion often become the demons of the succeeding one.

In the case of the Devil, it is only fair to add that though his genealogy has been subjected to considerable tampering, his place of residence, somewhere deep in the bowels of the earth, has not changed throughout all these years. Only people's attitude toward it has.

From being originally the home of the ancestors, the underworld became the home of sundry rebellious Titans, giants, Empusas, ghouls, vampires and monsters, as well as the usual crowd of dead souls in classical times, and finally ended up under Christian dispensation as a fiery pit of torment reserved for sinners and enemies of the church. Its management was seen to by those deposed gods and goddesses of antiquity whom the church could not quite assimilate into its framework.

It is to this home of the ancestors that shamans descended to rescue the souls of sick patients from the clutches of death. In order to gain ease of entrance and exit, they must first come to terms with those in charge down there.

In medieval Christianity the descent into the underworld—by Jesus, in this instance—became known as "the harrowing of hell." We shall be exploring that theme more closely in the next card. For now, let us devote our attention to those who actually

Figure 54

ruled the underworld and received the brunt of that harrowing. Who, in fact, is the Devil?

The Devil shown in most tarot decks is the familiar medieval one with goat's or bull's horns, bat's wings and either a trident, a pitchfork or a torch grasped in its hand (see Frontispiece). The bat's wings are in all probability a Christian addition stemming from the Judaic tradition that Satan was originally a fallen angel; good angels had white dove's wings, bad angels had leathery, batlike ones. The trident or its pitchfork variant is, like Zeus' thunderbolt, a symbol of death-dealing Titanic power. In Greek mythology it was wielded by Poseidon, the god of the sea, Zeus' third brother. It also appears in Indian mythology as one of the weapons of Shiva, the god of destruction. The horned animal theme we have already explored. It was a symbol of divine potency.

The Marseilles deck and some modern Italian tarots show the Devil wearing a version of the traditional shamanic helmet with stag's horns sprouting on either side (see Figure 54). He is often accompanied by two lesser devils, also wearing antlered hats. They are each chained by the neck to a ring fixed to the base of the pedestal on which the devil stands.

Sometimes the central figure is shown with satyrlike cloven feet, more often with eagle's claws, the relevance of which will become apparent when we study the magical nota from which the tarot card derives some of its symbolism.

A. E. Waite's tarot Devil borrows heavily from the visions of Eliphas Levi and shows him as a goat-legged, four-horned Goat of Mendes on whose brow burns the evil reversed pentagram— according to the occultism of Levi, the symbol of depravity.

This Goat of Mendes, theoretically an Egyptian form of Pan, has been lovingly dwelt on first by Levi and then by his followers, often linked with the mysterious idol Baphomet, supposedly worshiped by the ill-fated Knights Templar of the fourteenth century. That Baphomet has much to do with the Devil trump is probably a correct assumption, as we shall presently see; but that the Goat of Mendes had anything to do with the matter is very difficult to prove.

It is said that Baphomet himself appears carved on one of the doors of the baptistery in Florence; if the figure is indeed he, then he is probably indentifiable with none other than Janus, the god of doorways, which would seem reasonable enough in view of Janus' practice of guiding the destinies of individuals and whirling the wheel of fortune.

However, to find a more specific identification for the tarot Devil, we must turn our gaze to an obscure deity of a warrior cult mentioned more than once already: the cult of Mithra. We saw how the young solar hero Mithra latterly became equated with the god Dionysus; how Mithraic mysticism came to blend closely with that of Orphism. Mithra-Dionysus came to be worshiped as the *sol invictus*, "unconquered sun," who defied the toils of the underworld to be reborn each year at the winter solstice on the night of December 24. But before being reborn, the young hero had first to slay the bull, the spilling of whose magical blood ensured the defeat of the god of darkness, Ahriman. But Ahriman was only a regent of the despotic god of time himself, known to the Persian Mithraists as Zervan, to the Romans as Saturn. In this curious mixture of different religions which was the fabric of Mithraism, a somewhat familiar pattern thus begins to emerge, embodying at base the rotation of the seasons and the rebirth of life.

Very little is known about what the medieval Knights Templar actually believed. Accounts of their strange cult vary considerably from teller to teller; a large proportion of them are highly suspect, being obtained by the Inquisition through torture. But certain consistent elements do appear, though whether these were foisted by Inquisitors upon the knights is difficult to tell.

According to one account, Baphomet, the idol of the inner order of the Templars, was worshiped in the shape of a cat. Though cat-worship was a stock charge leveled at any heretic in those days, there may well have been something to it in the case of the Templars, as we shall see presently.

Statues of Baphomet were also often said to consist simply of a disembodied head which paradoxically possessed feet. A certain French monk, Deodatus Jaffet, and two Italian Templars presented similar testimony: that at their reception into the order they were instructed to adore the head as their god and mahomet, and worship it by kissing its feet.

Now in the Middle Ages "mahomet," "maumet," "mommet" or even "mammet" was a name borrowed from Mohammed, the prophet of Islam, by the Crusaders and applied to any kind of idol or little magical figurine. Witches used it on occasions as an alternative to "poppet" (from the Latin *puppa*, "a doll") to describe their wax hexing-dolls. It is more than likely that the name "Baphomet," rather than translating, as various occultists have proposed, as an unwieldy anagram of "father of the temple of universal peace," "baptism of wisdom" or even "stone of Buffo," simply came from a corruption of "mahomet," meaning "an idol."

But if "Baphomet" simply meant an idol, what god did it

Figure 55

represent? According to the Roman Church, it was quite obviously Satan himself. But since when has the Satan of Christianity been portrayed as a skull?—for that is how this Templar
head appeared in certain instances.

At other times it was carved to represent an old man with a
long beard. Sometimes the head possessed eyes "glowing like
carbuncles." Occasionally the head was that of a cat, sometimes
with one or more supernumerary faces attached.

As if this were not bizarre enough, Templar initiates indulged
in the odd practice of binding this idol with the magical cingula,
or cords, which they wore around their waists, in the belief that
this in some way induced fertility and brought luck.* Where can
we find a god like this?

The Mithraic god Zervan, Saturn, represents cosmic time. His
image was a terrifying one; he had the body of a man entwined
by a serpent (see Figure 55). Sometimes his legs terminated in

*See Thomas Wright, "The Worship of the Generative Powers," in *Sexual Symbolism*
(New York, Bell Publishing Co., 1957).

Figure 56

either cloven feet or birds' claws (as in the Mithraic relief from Modena) and wings sprouted from his shoulders. Either a blazing torch or a key was clutched in one hand and a staff in the other; or he brandished a reversed torch, as in the statue of Castel Gandolfo. Most dreadful of all was his head, which, when it was not that of a man, was that of a huge lion with gaping jaws (see Figure 56). In the event of the head being a man's, it was often crowned with a solar aureole from which sprang two curling horns, while out of his chest would stare the displaced cat's face, or alternatively the thunderbolt symbol common to Greek and Eastern iconography. Roman reliefs sometimes show fiery breath issuing from the lion-god's mouth. In fact, a statue from Sidon in the Middle East has the head hollowed out in such a manner that a fire may be lit within it to blaze fearsomely through the eyes, nostrils and mouth.

Zervan's Gnostic counterpart, the time god Ialdabaoth, was also sometimes given a cat's head. Alternatively he was represented as multiheaded, and it is this image which appears in

Agrippa's book of magic* as one of the spirits of Saturn: a tall, lean figure with four faces—one before, one behind, and one on either side, and, in addition, one on each knee. A fifteenth-century manuscript[†] portrays a similar figure but entitles it "The Prince of Darkness"—a very good title for him, recalling that of Hades, "the Invisible One."

In view of this evidence, it may well be that some of the Templars practiced a lingering remnant of the military cult of Mithra; it would certainly be a cult natural to them. Their mahomet was Saturn, the fearsome god of time himself, whose eyes glowed like carbuncles and whose symbol, among others, was a skull. The binding of such mahomets with cords may have been a simulation of the constriction of the zodiacal serpent around Zervan's body. The cord itself would then have been a variant of the magical tree or cosmic ladder, like Ariadne's thread.

A vision of this eternal tyrant, whether he was called Hades or Saturn, must have been encountered by Orphic and Mithraic initiates alike on their descent into the world of shadows. It is undoubtedly this erstwhile terror which now stares quaintly out at us from the tarot deck as the Devil.

When he appears in a tarot spread he is said to symbolize something totally inexorable, an occurrence which there is absolutely no possibility of ignoring. Naturally, for he is fate at its most tyrannous. When well aspected, this may be a happy event, but when reversed or badly placed, not so happy. Unlike the situation encountered with the Wheel of Fortune or the Hermit, the Devil allows you no choice in the matter. It is—or, rather, will be—totally out of your hands. How you can react or adapt yourself to it is, of course, another situation altogether.

---

*Heinrich Cornelius Agrippa von Nettesheim, *Fourth Book of Occult Philosophy* reprinted in J. Scheible, *Das Kloster* (Stuttgart, 1846).
†Illustration from illuminated ms. *Miniature of the Holy Grail* (Bibliothèque Nationale, Paris, fifteenth-century ms.).

The Tower

Fear him who was
immolated in Isaac
sold in Joseph
slain in the lamb
crucified in man
and then was triumphant over hell. . . .*

These words are taken from the old Roman Catholic ritual of exorcism for banishing an evil spirit, and the demon is enjoined to depart in the name of "him who . . . was triumphant over hell . . . " But Jesus was not the first or the last to harrow hell, as we have seen. It is and was the basic shamanic and Orphic goal.

Trump number sixteen in modern decks is usually labeled the Lightning-Struck Tower, which is simply a bald description of the picture shown: that of a tower with the battlements apparently set ablaze by a bolt of lightning. From the windows small bodies of men and women drop, either flung by the force of the concussion or hurling themselves out in a desperate attempt to escape the fire (see Figure 57).

French and Italian titles for this card are more informative. *La Maison Dieu* has led some tarot speculators to believe that the ruined building is none other than the temple of Jerusalem, either that of Solomon or the model destroyed centuries later during the Roman occupation. However, the word *Dieu*, "God," is a corruption, as one may see if one consults early packs, where *Diefel* appears instead. So quite the reverse interpretation applies: it is "the devil's house."

Another old name for the Tower is *L'Hospital*. Rather than translating as "the hospital," this is much more likely to refer directly back to the Latin root of the word, *hospes*, a host.

*"Rituale Romanum," exorcism ceremony of Pope Paul V.

Figure 57

"The Hostelry" would, therefore, seem to be a much more appropriate rendering, probably deriving from the ironic classical notion that the souls of the dead were in fact the guests of King Hades. The early Italian Bembo deck corroborates this idea, for the title attached to the card is simply "the Castle of Pluto."

In medieval art, the giant gaping lion's jaws of the god of time became the conventional representation of the underworld, Hellmouth. In between the large teeth an assortment of devils would usually be shown engaged in tormenting the souls of the damned (as the dead had become), while often in the center would sit Satan himself, or alternatively his Roman precursor, Pluto.*

Another fifteenth-century Italian title for this trump, *La Sagitta*, "The Arrow," may well refer to the lightning bolt itself, forking down upon the dark tower's battlements.

*See *Le Livre des echecs amoureux* (Bibliothèque Nationale, Paris, Catalogue No. ms. fr. 143), for an illustration of this.

Where are we to find a reference to this archaic overthrow of power, this devil's house struck by fire? To the cabalist, Sodom and Gomorrah, Atlantis or the Tower of Babel usually suggest themselves as possible interpretations. But as we are looking for a specifically pagan derivation, none of these references will really do.

Casting around for classical cataclysmic overthrows, we are of course inexorably led to the most obvious one of all: the great cosmic rebellion exemplified by such myths as the overthrow of Ouranos by Kronos, Kronos by Zeus, Set by Horus, Ahriman by Mithra and Hera's Titans by Dionysus.

The harrowing of hell—this resounding defeat of the powers of darkness—is, like all the other tarot stories, fundamental in myth and epic. It was also an essential element in the shaman's quest.

The Tower seems to derive its symbolism principally from the last cults mentioned, those of Mithra and Dionysus. Mithra defeats the powers of darkness by slaying the divine bull, which scholars think represented Ahriman himself, while others theorize that it was a symbol for the sun, Mithra's alter ego offered up to fate in a type of self-immolation like Odin's.

Dionysus, on the other hand, latterly closely linked with Mithra, is himself torn to pieces by jealous Hera's Titans. They are blasted by divine lightning for this sacrilege, and Dionysus rises again like the phoenix from the ashes. By a more long-winded account, he is born to Semele-Persephone after she has been impregnated by a potion made from his heart.

Both myths illustrate the mystery of the rebirth of life at the end of winter.

Though Dionysus himself dies in the course of his struggle with the powers of darkness, he is reborn through the intervention of his father, Zeus. Hell is split open by the divine lightning, and Dionysus is always reborn as Iacchus, Phosphorus Aster, from the fiery ruin of his enemies, even as the bull sacrifice of Mithra always announced the return of spring in May. Though a simple enough tale to recount now, this was at one time looked upon as the inmost secret of the Mysteries.

Hippolytus, a Christian apologist writing in the third century, brought it to light in a disparaging manner, chiefly because of its obvious similarity with that of the newly burgeoning Christian cult.

Apparently the Telesterion, temple of the Mysteries, was furnished with a chimneylike funnel on its roof, at the base of which lay a concealed furnace. The high point of the Mystery drama was reached when the officiating hierophant sang these words at midnight: "The Mistress has given birth to a Holy Boy! Brimo has given birth to Brimos! . . . "

As the cry went up, fire and smoke would belch forth from the chimney, lighting up the assembled celebrants with its radiance. Brimo, another name for Persephone, had brought Dionysus to birth once more. It is this mystical fact that constituted the initiatory experience of the Orphic illuminate.

The divine lightning which killed the Titan murderers of Dionysus was the same fire from which he himself was reborn. Both of Dionysus' births, by Semele and by Persephone, are accompanied by divine fire. In the first instance it consumes his mortal mother, Semele; in the second, it destroys his Titan murderers.

The power of darkness, that old god of time, who is an image of the Fool himself, perishes in the flames and the new god is born from them—the Fool reborn. The story is nothing less than the prototype for Marcos' Gnostic creed, and the theories of the alchemists, for that matter: the renovation of dead matter by divine fire.

Though the trappings change from country to country, it is an extremely ancient idea, probably responsible for the old European practice of lighting solstitial balefires every year, through which people would leap and cattle be driven. Christianity preserved these rituals in those customs of lighting the paschal candle and yule log. In the same way that Demeter tries to immortalize her foster child Demophon, Dionysus is reborn in the flames after his confrontation with the powers of darkness; similarly, Mithra, the sun, is reborn from the burning earth at the winter solstice.

It is this descent of divine lightning into the underworld which is portrayed in the Lightning-Struck Tower. To both Christian and pagan it implied the harrowing of hell, which meant the defeat of winter and the powers of darkness. It heralded the rebirth of light.

When it appears in a tarot spread, it is said to signify a baptism of fire, a personal cataclysmic event leading to good or bad, depending on its orientation and your intuition. In modern terms it would indicate a catharsis rather than total ruin. The Old Man dies; the new is reborn from the flames.

The Star

The brightest "star" in the sky known to the ancients was the planet which we today call Venus. The Greeks knew it as Hesperus in the evening and Phosphorus in the morning, for it made two nightly appearances, just after sunset and immediately prior to the dawn. The Romans translated Phosphorus as Lucifer, the *stella matutina*. In Hebrew it was known as *Helel ben Sahar*—that is, "Day Star, Son of the Morning." In addition to morning star and evening star, Venus was also the lodestar or guiding light, and according to the Saxons it was originally a boatman named Earendil or Orvendill who had been set to shine in the night sky as a guide to those in greatest darkness.

Most importantly in our context, "Phosphorus Aster," Morning Star, was the title bestowed by the Greeks upon Iacchus, the reborn Dionysus.

Figure 58

The present-day tarot of Bologna, following the lead of the Florentine Minchiate, presents this trump as a vignette of the three Magi, those wise kings of the East who followed the Star of Bethlehem in search of the infant Jesus. Most French decks, however—including that of Waite—take their inspiration from the Marseilles tarot and show a nude woman kneeling by a pool pouring the contents of two pitchers into the water before her. In the background grows a tree or bush; above burns the same enormous star surrounded by a glittering array of lesser ones (see Figure 58). Tarot commentators have speculated that this represents Ganymede or Aquarius. It is very similar to the figure of Temperance. However, the fortune-teller's traditional meanings for the card—hope, gifts, guidance, healing, regeneration—do not really seem to jibe with this interpretation. They seem to be related more to the alternative Three Wise Kings design for the card.

To find out who the lady is we must turn our gaze eastward, to the goddesses of Mesopotamia. Three of the symbols most common in ancient Babylonian hieratic texts are those of the Star, the Moon and the Sun. The Star is invariably associated with the great Sumerian goddess Inanna, who later became Ishtar and Astarte, that ancient "abomination" whose worship was to periodically plague the Old Testament prophets later on. She may also be linked with the Persian Manichean deity Anahita—in Greek, Anaitis—who in turn was worshiped as a goddess of the regenerative waters that flow from "behind the region of the Summer Stars."*

An interesting tale is told of the Emperor Julian, the so-called apostate nephew of Constantine, who tried to turn the world back to paganism in the fourth century A.D. When passing in triumph through Antioch, today's Turkey, he was much gratified to find the assembled pagan populace hailing him as the "Star of Salvation, dawning in the East," which he took to refer to himself in his self-imposed office as reinstator of the old pagan cults. However, the truth of the matter lay deeper than

*See Cumont, *Recherches sur le Manicheisme* (Brussels, 1908).

that. For the people of Antioch, the "Star of Salvation, dawn-ing in the East" was, of course, the planet Venus; its early morning rising signaled the arrival of the goddess Astarte to waken Adonis, the Eastern Dionysus, from the tomb on his great festival day each year. It was thus a symbol of reawaken-ing and rebirth, a highly appropriate title for Julian in pagan eyes. We can see that the Star of Bethlehem carried the same meaning, for it was also a sign of salvation and renewal. It is possible that the woman depicted on the Star was once the great goddess herself, come to greet her lord on his return from the underworld.

The star of Inanna is presented in ancient inscriptions as an eight-pointed one; it is similarly depicted in the Marseilles deck. On the other hand, the pentacle, five-pointed, appears on many decks also. It was an equally ancient derivation, also appearing in Mesopotamian and Greek inscriptions as a potent magical symbol.

In arcane lore the pentacle is known by a great assortment of titles: a goblin's foot; *Drudenfuss*, or druid's foot; pentalpha; pentagram; Star of Bethlehem; Star of the Magi; and Three Kings' Star. In Arthurian legend it was the Star of Logres, the emblem of Arthur's kingdom; in Templar and Masonic lore, the Star in the East or Blazing Star. Even as Isis once protected the infant Horus from the wrath of Set, Ariadne kept Theseus from the fury of the Minotaur and Astarte preserved Tammuz from the wiles of Nergal and Ereshkigal. The five-pointed star has remained a symbol of rebirth, protection and salvation. It has been traced upon doorsteps and worn upon the breasts of the students of *grimoires* as protection against the powers of dark-ness from time immemorial.

When used as a symbol of protection, the pentacle is frequently embellished with mysterious cabalistic sigils and words of power, such as "Tetragrammaton." Though the penta-cle as a symbol dates back to pre-cabala days, these additional fortifications are definitely Judaic in origin, being drawn from a Christianized cabala common in Northern Europe during the Middle Ages.

Figure 59

The symbols within the points of the star were originally Hebrew lettering (see Figure. 59). The pentacle itself was often referred to as the Three Kings' Star, and the kings referred to are, of course, the Magi who came to pay homage to the newborn Jesus and warn his parents of Herod's plan. According to one legend, the kings came from the town which is now Cologne.

Melchior (coming from *melech*, meaning "king") was said to have brought frankincense as a deity offering; Gaspar (from *yashpeh*, the precious stone jasper) brought embalming myrrh; and Balthazar (from *baal shasar*, lord of treasures) brought gold to "crown him again."

Another legend claims that the three Magi hailed from a Samaritan tribe known as the Cutheans, a race given to wizardry, whose roots stretched far back into prehistory and who, according to Talmudic traditions, shared a common ancestry with the gypsies! In fact, in European legend the Three Wise Kings themselves are often thought of as gypsies.

The symbols in the pentacle points may well represent the

words *abdia, bellony* and *bellator* (or *ballaton*), which in turn are probably the battered remnants of Gaspar, Melchior (frequently misspelled as "Belchior") and Balthazar. The equally mysterious *hallii hra* and *halliza* are all that is left of the German *Heilig Heilig Heilig* ("Holy Holy Holy"), and the potent *Soluzen* once was simply *Elohim*, "God."

In addition to being worn as a protective talisman, the pentacle was also traced with consecrated chalk on the floor within the boundary of a circle. When under magical attack or if dealing with particularly dangerous spirits the wizard would stand within this diagram for protection. According to an eighteenth-century German calabistic *grimoire, The Magical Kabala of the Sixth and Seventh Books of Moses*, each line of the pentacle should measure exactly thirteen feet. Upon kneeling within the star facing east, the names of the Magi—Gaspar, Melchior and Balthazar—should each be called upon by the wizard, followed by an invocation of the word of power, "*Elohim*" 375 times. Greater power would be added to the invocation if the planets Jupiter, Mars and Saturn, representing the Three Kings, were above the horizon and the ceremony performed at new or full Moon. Which of the latter times was chosen would depend on what type of spirits were being summoned, good or evil.

The landscape itself of the Star trump may contain a certain significance. In medieval miracle or Mystery plays, one of the stock scenic features was an area of the stage which represented the sea, always set next to the section representing Hellmouth. It could be used to "sail" on and represent long journeys to outremer and the ends of the earth; and it could also be dipped into by Lazarus to wet the tongue of suffering Dives.

However, this concept of a mysterious hellish pool may go back much further to another ancient Greek idea concerning the underworld. Within the twilight kingdom of Hades there were two pools in addition to the numerous rivers, which included the Styx, Phlegethon, Lethe and Cocytus among others. One was the Pool of Forgetfulness, fed by the waters of the river Lethe, and the other, lying to the right of it, the Pool of Memory. In the foreground of the Star design one of these pools may be represented. Undoubtedly it would be that of Mnemosyne, Memory, which the goddess replenishes and the Orphic initiate drinks from before he leaves the underworld in order not to forget his mystical experience when he returns to the world above.

When the Star appears in your tarot layout it is thought to be an excellent sign, whatever its orientation. It signifies hope, rebirth and healing, a new promise of life and salvation. It also forecasts gifts and joy, for it hails the rebirth of Dionysus.

The Moon

Hell has been conquered. After defeating the Devil, whether identified as Set, Ialdaboath, Saturn or Hades, the initiate Fool has by the grace of the goddess, Isis, Sophia, or Persephone, been given an underworld rebirth as Osiris, Dionysus or Mithra. The names of the gods differ from place to place; the Mystery remains the same.

With the Star, the reborn initiate began his reascent, which takes him into the heavens themselves where the same underworld gods that he has already encountered will be revealed to him in their radiant celestial aspects.

> If you read the second formula [of the Book of Thoth] even if you are in the tomb, you will resume the form you had on earth; you will even see the sun rising in the sky with his following of gods, and the moon in the form she takes to appear. . . .*

Undoubtedly this "formula" refers to the same initiation experience mentioned by Lucius Apuleius and quoted earlier:

> . . . I approached the limits of the dead; I trod upon the threshold of Proserpina [the Roman Persephone] and I was carried beyond the spheres of the elements. I . . . approached the Gods of the Underworld, and those from On High; and I worshipped them face to face. . . .

The Moon, the second of the greater trumps, is the next heavenly phenomenon to be witnessed by the initiate after the Star (see Figure 60).

Various Gnostic papyri still preserve rituals similar to the one referred to by the Book of Thoth, whereby the initiate could

*"The Story of Ptah-nefer-ka," Ptolemaic papyrus. See Wallis Budge, *Egyptian Magic* (New York, University Bks., no date), pp. 143-46, and Serge Sauneron, *The Priests of Ancient Egypt* (London, Evergreen Bks. Ltd., 1960), p. 123.

open the heavens after besting the powers of the underworld. Frequently identifying the initiate with the "new man" Jesus, these Gnostic scripts represent the Moon and the Sun as boats or chariots manned by their ruling deities.

Figure 60

Essentially there are three phases of the Moon, and each was seen by the ancients as one face of the Great Goddess, of Many Names. The thin, pale white crescent of the New Moon was "the Maiden"—chaste Persephone, Artemis or Athena—the sprouting grain. The Full Moon, hanging red over the harvest fields, was "the Lady"—bride and mother Demeter, Isis, Astarte—the time of reaping. Lastly, the Dark Moon was "the Hag"—sinister Hecate and jealous Juno, envious Ereshkigal eager to reclaim what she regarded as her own—the sowing or "burial" of the grain.

Most modern tarot trumps simply show the Moon's disc as the central figure. Only when we study earlier packs like the Bembo deck do we find the goddess represented in person, in this instance as the classical Diana holding a crescent Moon in her hands.

Other designs feature a pair of astrologers measuring the height of the Moon's ascension with a pair of calipers or a man serenading his true love on a balcony, beneath the Moon.

Nowadays, decks which feature a central lunar disc, often with a face—all that is left of the goddess, in fact—also depict mysterious flecks or drops falling from it. These are interpreted by some as drops of blood or by others more cabalistically inclined as "yods" (Hebrew letter "i" or "j"—the first letter of the Tetragrammaton). In all probability they simply represent dew drops, which were once thought to be drawn up and let fall through the influence of the Moon.

Flanking the Moon, staring up at it, two baying dogs are usually shown—all that is left of Diana's pack of hounds, those hell-hounds that guard the ways in and out of the underworld.*

Two pillars or towers stand beyond the dogs, framing the picture. They are interpreted by more Rosicrucian-minded occultists as Egyptian pylons representing the cabalistic pillars of severity and mercy, Jachin and Boaz, on the tree of life; by others as megalithic menhirs or standing-stones. They are more likely to represent the twin pillars of Hercules, which were once thought to have stood on either side of the Straits of Gibraltar. To the primitive mind the uncharted waters beyond may well have seemed to conceal one of the ways down to the underworld, possibly via the country of the Hyperboreans, that "land behind the North Wind."

In the foreground of the trump lies another pond; maybe it is the Pool of Forgetfulness or simply all that is left of the Mediterranean. Or else it is just a dew pond from which dew drops rise and fall. Out of it crawls what appears to be a crayfish; originally it was probably a crab, which according to astrology is the zodiacal sign governed by the Moon. This is more than likely, seeing that the crab forms part of the magical nota which provided the inspiration for this trump.

---

*The entrance to the Vedic underworld, the Realm of Yama, like that of the Greeks and the Celts, significantly enough was also guarded by two hounds. It is a familiar mythological motif.

Agrippa mentions a picture of a "many-footed insect"—
which could include anything from a spider to a centipede—in
his list of possible lunar images. But, more specifically, he
recommends for fertility, children's health and an antidote to
poisons a talisman composed when the Moon ascended in the
first ten degrees of Cancer. The image was to be that of a
horned woman riding either a bull, a seven-headed dragon or a
crab. She should, moreover, be depicted grasping a dart in her left
hand, a looking glass in the right, and be clad in white or
green. Two serpents should rise on either side of her horned
headdress and twine about her arms and legs.* Vincenzo Cartari, the Renaissance iconographer, mentions a similar image,
naming it correctly as Isis, the Egyptian Moon goddess.†

The dart is all that is left of her scepter and the looking glass
of her sistrum, the sacred loop-shaped rattle. The serpent motif
on arms and legs seems to have been incorporated from the
ancient Minoan mountain mother. The child whose health Isis
originally watched over was Horus, her own son.

But by far the best description of the goddess that we have
comes from Lucius Apuleius, and it is worth quoting in full, for
it, or a similar one, undoubtedly provided the original for
Agrippa's and Cartari's image:

> ... Her long thick hair fell in tapering ringlets on her lovely neck,
> and was crowned with an intricate chaplet in which was woven every
> kind of flower. Just above her brow shone a round disc, like a
> mirror, or like the bright face of the Moon, which told me [Lucius]
> who she was. Vipers** rising from the left-hand and right-hand
> partings of her hair supported this disc, with ears of corn bristling
> beside them. Her many-colored robe was of finest linen; part was
> glistening white, part crocus-yellow, part glowing red and along the
> entire hem a woven bordure of flowers and fruit clung swaying in
> the breeze. But what caught my eye more than anything else was the
> deep black lustre of her mantle. She wore it slung across her body

---

*Heinrich Cornelius Agrippa, von Nettesheim, *Occult Philosophy* in J. Scheible, *Das Kloster* (Stuttgart, 1846).
†Vincenzo Cartari, *Le Imagini colla sposizione degli dei degli antichi* (Venice, Marcolini, 1556).
**Uraei, the sacred snakes of Egypt with which gods and royalty were crowned.

from the right hip to the left shoulder, where it was caught in a knot resembling the boss of a shield; but part of it hung in innumerable folds, the tasseled fringe quivering. It was embroidered with glittering stars on the hem and everywhere else, and in the middle beamed a full and fiery moon.

In her right hand she held a bronze rattle [sistrum], of the sort used to frighten away the God of the Sirocco; its narrow rim was curved like a sword-belt and three little rods, which sang shrilly when she shook the handle, passed horizontally through it. A boat-shaped gold dish hung from her left hand, and along the upper surface of the handle writhed an asp ready to strike. On her divine feet were slippers of palm leaves, the emblem of victory. . . . *

Isis' answer to Lucius' prayer which follows this description has an interesting preamble which explains the entire syncretist thesis:

. . . Though I am worshipped in many aspects, known by countless names, and propitiated with all manner of different rites, yet the whole round earth venerates me. The primeval Phrygians call me Pessinuntica, Mother of the Gods; the Athenians, sprung from their own soil, call me Cecropian Artemis; for the islanders of Cyprus I am Paphian Aphrodite; for the archers of Crete I am Dictynna;† for the trilingual Sicilians, Stygian Proserpine; and for the Eleusians their ancient Mother of the Corn.**

Some know me as Juno, some as Bellona of the Battles;†† others as Hecate, others again as Rhamnubia,*** but both races of Aethiopians, whose lands the morning sun shines upon, and the Egyptians who excel in ancient learning and worship me with ceremonies proper to my godhead, call me by my true name, namely, Queen Isis. . . . †††

In Lucius' vision, the goddess appears to rise from the sea and hang poised and radiant above the surface of the waves like her celestial symbol, the Full Moon. The tarot Moon likewise repre-

*Lucius Apuleius, *The Golden Ass,* trans. by Robert Graves (London, Penguin Books, 1950), p. 270.
†A version of Cyrene and Autonoë.
**Demeter.
††Roman female counterpart to Mars.
***Possibly a version of Nemesis, goddess of fate.
†††Lucius Apuleuis, *The Golden Ass,* trans. by Robert Graves (London. Penguin, 1950), p. 271.

sents the goddess resplendent in the heavens, reflected in the waters below.

In ancient Greek myth, the Moon was also closely connected with Medusa, one of three sisters known as the Gorgons. She mated with Poseidon, the dark god of the sea; as a consequence of performing the marriage act in Athena's temple, the goddess gave her face the basilisk quality of turning mortals to stone if they so much as looked at it. Whether this power came from her beauty or the mane of hissing serpents that Athena turned her hair into no one knows. In any event, Athena had no love for Medusa. Because of this, Athena lent Perseus her shield to use as a mirror and thus avoid the death-dealing glance. With the aid of the winged sandals of Hermes, the hero flew into the Gorgon's cave and, gazing into the shield to make sure of his aim, cut off Medusa's head.

The disembodied head of Medusa was sent by Persephone to greet unwarranted intruders into the underworld. Apparently she shared it with Athena, for it was also sported as a central boss on Athena's shield. Persephone and Athena seem to have been different aspects of the same goddess by all accounts. Indeed, Medusa herself seems to have been the great goddess' terrible alter ego, for the word "gorgoneion" was used by Orphic initiates to describe the lunar disc. Undoubtedly the three Gorgon sisters symbolized the three phases of the Moon, new, full and dark, "beheaded" by the sickle every month.

There is, of course, an immense amount of mystical lore connected with the Moon inasmuch as she is traditionally the mistress of all classical witches.

The legend of Perseus introduced a notion important to Moon magic: the idea of reflection. Mirrors, quartz crystals and pieces of glass have always been intimately associated with the Moon; like water and silvery metals, they all reflect. The Moon itself is a mirror, and Isis wore one on her brow. One of the most constantly repeated allegations which appear in connection with witchcraft, from archaic Greece through the classical period right up into the Middle Ages, is that the practitioner can actually "draw the Moon down" from the sky. In view of the initiate's mystical acquaintanceship with the Moon, this extravagant claim appears to be based on psychic experience if not physical fact. But besides this occult definition, the term also may point to the practice of simply enlarging, and therefore "drawing down" the image of the lunar disc in a mirrorlike shield or globular lens, or, simpler still, in an empty bowl. It is just possible that a development of this early scientific discovery was made use of—possibly by means of a rudimentary camera obscura—as part of the Mystery initiation to "draw down" the Full Moon image into the precincts of the telesterion itself and present it to the wondering, semientranced gaze of the initiate.

The Moon not only ruled all reflecting surfaces but also all water. A connection between the phases of the Moon and the sea tides was made very early in history. The living tide, the flux of blood experienced in the female menstrual cycle, also came to be looked upon as governed by the Moon in a similar manner.

Many people today still believe that the Moon exerts some deep-seated occult influence on human behavior. If there is any truth to the observation, it may have some link to the possibly hormonally induced physiological responses recorded by an American psychiatrist, Dr. Curt Richter, among his patients at the Johns Hopkins Hospital in Baltimore, Maryland. Many of them appeared to register a periodic cycle of normal/abnormal behavior over a period of twenty-eight days—the lunar month. However, whether the Moon itself triggered this activity was not ascertained. Certainly the ancients considered abnormal activity directly attributable to the Moon's influence, as the very word "lunacy" attests. The myth of the werewolf with his built-in lunar triggering device springs partially from this old belief. That dogs do howl at the Moon does seem to be a fact. That certain animals—notably aquatic ones like oysters, eels and mudworms—mysteriously register the transit of the Moon overhead, even indoors with no tidal conditions present, was established by Dr. Frank Brown of Northwestern University at Evanston, Illinois, in 1953. So maybe there is, as modern astrologers would have us believe, more to the old occult myth of lunar influence than mere association of ideas.

Various herbs also share a traditional affiliation with the

Moon. The Artemisias rank high on this list. Their name itself is a sure indicator, deriving from that of Artemis, the classical Moon goddess. The juice of the mugwort, one of the Artemisias, was once used to anoint magical mirrors and lenses to impart divinatory virtue to them.

Another herb which according to modern occultists falls under this lunar heading is aloeswood (sweet aloes, not bitter). Lily and jasmine are also sometimes considered lunar perfumes, as are the white rose and the aromatic essence camphor. Pomegranates, no doubt through their associations with Persephone and Juno, are also lunar—they provide a background to the High Priestess trump in the Waite deck. In Italian witchcraft, the lemon is sacred to the Moon and is closely associated with the Judaic Succoth *ethrog*.

Most modern tarot interpretations of the Moon trump follow the negative line of thought present in the word "lunacy." Deception" and "twilight error" are often attached as meanings to the upright card, with the interpretation mitigated as "fluctuation" and "small errors" where reversed. This would be a reasonable interpretation of the Dark Moon; but actually we have three faces to choose from, the New Moon, like the Star, indicating promise and the Full Moon fertility and fulfillment.

The trump may best be read as "fluctuation" when it appears in a layout; whether from good to bad or vice versa must be intuited by the reader. It is a feminine archetype, however, and this should be borne in mind when reading it: it implies a gentle inner fluctuation rather than that violent fiery catharsis of the Tower or the worldly swing of the Wheel.

The Sun

This is a trump about which there is very little disagreement. The Moon rules the night and the Sun rules the day. Having confronted the deity of the Moon, the new Orphic initiate continues his heavenly ascent and confronts the god of the Sun: his celestial master.

Card number nineteen, the third of the greater trumps, shows this "Sun behind the Sun," as the Neoplatonists knew him—the *sol invictus*, unconquered Sun Mithra, who amalgamated within himself the functions of earlier solar deities like Helios, Hyperion and classical Apollo, as well as the attributes of Dionysus.

The Sun's disc has always been associated with kingship and opulence throughout the world, whether the deity behind it was considered a wrathful or a beneficent one.

The talisman magic of Agrippa mentions a solar image for success, a crowned king who rests his feet upon a globe, while on his breast he nurses a raven. This is none other than Mithra, although Agrippa naturally does not say as much.* The sunburst itself still maintains this talismanic quality and is sported as the sign of more than one bank or insurance company. The Roman emperors came to identify themselves with the solar glory, as did Louis XIV, the "Sun King" of France.

In all tarot Suns the solar orb, or sunburst, is prominently displayed. In the Bembo pack, it is carried by a child or *putto*, possibly the youthful Mithra, Phaëthon or simply Sol. In most decks, however, the sunburst, like the Moon, blazes alone midheaven, staring blandly out of the card surrounded by a fiery nimbus (see Figure 61). Beyond this, drops of water again sometimes appear—this time probably representing the regular evaporation of seas and lakes which will condense to fall again as rain. On the ground a couple of youngsters play. In the

---

*It is undoubtedly drawn from the Picatrix image mentioned earlier.

Figure 61

Marseilles deck they are shown as children, possibly Gemini, the heavenly twins, or Dioscuri as the Greeks knew them. In Minchiate decks, however, they appear to have aged slightly and are depicted as two young lovers. Waite's deck simply shows a child seated on horseback carrying a standard: a variant upon one of the magical, cabalistic images of Tiphareth. For in the cabala, the Sun occupies a central position on the Tree of Life, directly above the Moon. Above the Sun, in turn, lies Kether, the Absolute. Thus cabalists Giordano Bruno and Waite saw the Sun as vice-regent of the Absolute, the outward visible sign of God.

Various traditionally treasure-guarding spirits derive from ancient solar myths, for the Sun governed the metal gold among other things. The dwarf Alberich and the demon Aciel were two of these beings.

Alberich was the malevolent dwarf who appears in the Teutonic epic of *Ring of the Nibelung*. The golden ring and treasure of the king of the dwarfs lay in his keeping. Siegfried, the hero of the epic, defeated Alberich in battle and took the ring for his own after demanding an oath of allegiance from the dwarf, only to have it wrested from his hands later.

Alberich's ancestry was a distant one, stretching far back to Vulcan and those volcano deities, the Hephaestoi. Aciel or Aziel (sometimes spelled Azael), on the other hand, was a favorite spirit of the "Faust books," eighteenth-century German *grimoires* whose general goal was the speedy enrichment of the conjurer. Whereas Alberich represented the lord of treasure's potential in romance, Aciel demonstrated his more practical uses! (See Figure 62.) His origins may be traced all the way back to the Babylonian Sun god, Shamash.

The Sun's birthday was, of course, the winter solstice, celebrated on December 25. When he shone brightly in the midsummer sky he was the mighty celestial god; but when he burned weakly and close to the horizon in winter, he was a dying one, soon to be reborn in fiery conflagration as a little child at the winter solstice.

The magical art of "drawing down the Sun" was once considered to be as special an ability as that of "drawing down the Moon." Instead of "catching" the image within a cup or bowl of liquid, the image of the midday Sun was concentrated by a lens or concave mirror and projected in a burning pinpoint upon dry tinder. In this manner a flame was lit. Fire was itself a valuable commodity in ancient times, and the fire derived from this process even more so, being known as elf, wild or need fire. Its primary use was to kindle festive bonfires, known as balefires, at the solstices and equinoxes, of which tradition the yule log, paschal candle and Guy Fawkes bonfire are the last remaining scraps. The flames were also considered to be a sure guard against the powers of evil. All European ritual purifications by fire appear to stem from the ancient tradition of passing people, animals and objects through these balefires as a means of warding off evil influences, just as ritual asperging by holy water may well stem from the baptismal washing of initiates. Fire produced by the friction of two pieces of wood also had the same magical value as solar fire; so did flames kindled by a

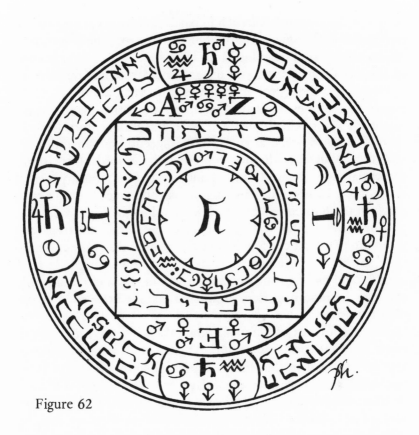

Figure 62

stroke of lightning. It was all celestial and, therefore, magically potent.

In European magic and witchcraft, solar things pertained to matters of joy and abundance, for unlike the case in torrid regions, the Sun was a source of light and life rather than heat and drought. The hotter the land, the less likely is the Sun to be welcomed as a beneficial deity. In northern climes it is the symbol of summer, and a good summer once meant everything to herdsmen and farmers.

Many of the "solar" plants of the medieval herbalist derived their associations through mythological ties. Others were connected by simpler associations. For example, the sunflower head not only resembled a sunburst but was also supposed to turn to face the Sun wherever it happened to be. The heliotrope, "sun-seeker," another solar plant, did likewise. The orange, on account of its shape and color, was a solar fruit. The sundew, a sinister little carnivorous marsh plant with extended spines, each tipped with its tiny globule of digestive "dew" in which unwary flies stick, was also solar.

But the most important solar plants were those with mythological associations, such as the mistletoe and bay, sacred to Balder and Apollo, Sun gods of Norse and classical pantheons. Both plants were held to be extremely efficacious in countering evil sorcery and for this reason were used as decorations at the winter solstice, to aid the Sun in its struggle with the powers of darkness.

St.-John's-wort had similar beneficent solar virtues but was used chiefly at the summer solstice, as were sprigs of angelica and vine leaves, holy to Dionysus. In keeping with the ancient traditions of astrology, for maximum effect these herbs were culled with a bronze sickle on the day of the Sun (Sunday), when the Sun itself was "angular" and therefore most potent, and preferably during those hours when it was above the horizon—that is at dawn, midday or sunset.

When the tarot Sun appears in a spread it is an obvious symbol of splendor and triumph, whether reversed or not. It may be interpreted as health, wealth or simply abundant joy, and its radiance is said to illuminate all the cards about it.

The Judgment

This card is sometimes known as the Resurrection or the Angel. It is the fourth of the greater trumps and usually depicts a winged angel hovering in the heavens sounding a trumpet. Below him the tombs and graves fly open, and the naked bodies of the dead rise to answer his summons, hands prayerfully clasped in front of them (see Figure 63).

In Christian terms, the greater trumps correspond to the last part of the Creed Mystery: " . . . He ascended into Heaven;/From thence He shall come to judge/The Quick and the Dead. . . ."

Figure 63

Although the deck of tarots painted by Bembo offers an exception to the rule, with a paternal God flanked by angels as the central tableau, most, including the Minchiate, follow the lead of the Marseilles pack and feature a single trumpeting angel. This is undoubtedly Saint Michael, the archangel, and he can be recognized as such if not by the action he performs, then by his traditional cross-emblazoned banner floating from the trumpet itself.

Now, as we have frequently noted, Christian saints and angels often took over the duties of pagan deities, generally with little more than a change of name and a symbol or two to make them fit in with the new religion. Saint Michael is no exception to the rule. His name simply translates "Who is like the Lord?" which is no real clue to his identity. We must turn to the cabala for help. Here Michael's ancestry is fully explained: he is one of the seven mighty archangels who guide the planets in their courses; in Michael's instance the planet was considered to be either the Sun or Mercury. In either role he is a fit wakener of the dead, either as the clear light of heaven or the angel of that planet, which according to astrological lore imparts benignity, motion and intelligence, elegance and consonance of speech.

Who better to awaken them?

The important identification, however, is that of Mercury, in classical mythology none other than our old friend Hermes Psychopomp, Guide of Souls. In this role, like Odin, Chooser of the Slain, and dark Anubis of Egypt, Michael leads the soul of the initiate into and out of the other world.

As Hermes began the procession of tarot trumps, so also does he end it. He is the mediator between the worlds, divine herald of the Mysteries. He guided the Fool's hand along the dark way into the world of shadows: " . . . This way. O come! Angel of the dead, Hermes, lead me on!"*

Now he leads him out again, reborn of Persephone and transformed. The Judgment shows the Orphic initiate's emergence from the grave "in Dionysus." "Why seek ye the living among the dead?" asked the angel of the mourning women come to anoint Jesus' body on the third day in the Christian version of the mystery. " . . . He is not here but risen!"

Behind this card of Resurrection also lies that mysterious

---

*Sophocles, *Oedipus at Colonus*, trans. by Robert Fitzgerald in *Sophocles, the Oedipus Cycle: An English Version.*

concept inherent in sophisticated Eastern religions like Buddhism and Vedanta but stemming from far earlier sources: the idea of reincarnation. Not only did the underworld rebirth guarantee an enlightenment in this life to the Mystery initiate, but it also ensured the additional bonus of being well placed in the next. For he who had already passed safely through the gates of death in the footsteps of his Lord and Lady once had little to fear a second time. Hence the Mystery initiate's odd lack of the fear of death, a phenomenon commented upon in many places by many writers.

Florentine witchcraft also appears to have maintained this belief in a future life upon earth. However, it was not looked on as a source of anguish, as it would be by an adherent of Buddhism, but rather as a further adventure. For like all shamans, the *strega* looked upon past and future lives as a source of power:

> Eman hetan! Eman hetan!
> I am of thee and thou art mine,
> I have nothing which is not thine.
> In thy name Lord,
> behold thy servant anointing himself!
> I should some day be great like thee!
> Thout a thout, thout, throughout and about!

Ultimately, as attested in this traditional anointing charm, the witch probably hoped to reach the stature and power of her master. As Diana and Lucifer walked the earth in mortal form to gain full mastery, so did the witch. Such progress would take time, possibly many lives, to attain; the only preference she showed on the subject of rebirth was that she be reborn among those whom she loved.*

When the Judgment appears in your tarot layout, it signifies the final determination of some matter, with the further suggestion of a new enterprise to follow. If it be reversed or badly aspected it often implies a reluctance to come to a conclusion or hesitation resulting in delay or postponement. It is, above all, a card of resolution and completion, signifying the final outcome.

*See C. G. Leland, *Estruscan Magic and Occult Remedies* (New York, University Books, 1963), pp. 199-202.

The World

We have now reached the last stage of the Mystery: that card known as the World or Universe, sometimes the Crown of the Magi. The Fool has reached the end of his quest.

The fifteenth-century Visconti deck of tarots painted by Bonifacio Bembo shows an untypical image of two cherubs supporting a globe in which is contained an elaborately towered castle. Its rocky foundations rise out of the waters of the sea. Overhead in the firmament the celestial fire of many stars glitters brightly. Thus the four elements are represented by sea, land, air and stars.

The fairy-tale castle or fortified city probably represents the heavenly Jerusalem, that holy city of God, which during the Middle Ages became the Christian equivalent of the classical garden of the Hesperides or Happy Isles; the Tir-an-og and Avalon of Celtic myth. It was the ideal state, like King Arthur's legendary Kingdom of Logres and later projected utopias like the cities of the Sun of Bacon or Bruno, who took their inspiration from Plato. In ancient times all cities took for their ground plan this archetype of Ozlike perfection.

Plutarch, writing on the "disciplina Etrusca," mentions the mysterious method by which the aboriginal Etruscans consecrated a city site. A circular trench known as a *mundus*, "world," was first dug in the center of the site. Into this were thrown first fruits, corn and libations of wine, milk and honey; then a stone or handful of native earth from the place which each man called home was also tossed in. Using the *mundus* as a pivotal center, an all-embracing circular trench was then plowed, to represent the city limit, using a bronze plowshare harnessed to a cow and a bull. Wherever a gateway was to be built, the plow was lifted and a gap left in the furrow. Any stones or clods or earth turned up by the plow were then

Figure 64

thrown back into the giant ring, a ritual reminiscent of the old magical practice of sweeping the dirt on a doorstep *toward* the house to keep the luck in. For the home, like the citadel and the temple, is holy ground, and the *mundus* is represented by the altar hearth.

A far more typical design for the World tarot trump is the one displayed on the Marseilles deck (see Figure 64).

A mandalalike wreath of leaves floats midheaven, bound in two places by flowers or ribbons—the "Crown of the Magi" itself. At the corners of the card the heads of the four holy living creatures of Ezekiel—lion, bull, man, and eagle—stare majestically out.

In medieval liturgical art these animals generally represented the four Aristotelian elements, the four corners of the earth, and the four Gospel-makers—Matthew, Mark, Luke and John. Matthew represented the element water, Mark fire, Luke earth, and John air. They were frequently shown as such on the four extremities of reliquary crucifixes.*

Because of their guardianship of the four directions, they

*Such as the reliquary cross of Heinrich von Wartenbach, C. 1200.

were often invoked in night spells to protect the sleeper from all harm: "Matthew, Mark, Luke and John/Bless this bed that I lie on!"

The cabala, calling on archangels rather than Christian saints, dealt with the same problem in a similar manner: "Before me Uriel,/Behind me Raphael/At my right Michael/At my left Gabriel!"

From this, we can trace the practice back to ancient Babylon: "Shamash before me,/Sin behind me/Nergal at my right,/Ninib at my left!"*

Within the wreath of the World stands what could be a young female or alternatively a youth from whose shoulders flutters a long scarf or stole. In one hand it carries a baton of sorts. Waite, following the lead of those French magi whom he himself was later to decry, places a rod in both hands. There is very little traditional justification for this. If anything at all were to be placed in the other hand it would be a crown, as shown in Florentine Minchiate decks. Who is this mysterious draped genius?

The French fortune-tellers' title of Crown of the Magi presents us with our first clue, referring either to the wreath itself or the crown grasped in the hand of the Minchiate figure. Our friend Lucius Apuleius, discoursing on the aftermath of his initiation, mentions this crown or chaplet in detail:

> The solemn rites ended at dawn and I emerged from the sanctuary. . . . The High Priest ordered me to mount into the wooden pulpit which stood in the center of the temple. . . . I was wearing an outer garment of fine linen embroidered with flowers, and a precious scarf hung down from my shoulders to my ankles. . . . The priests call this scarf an Olympian stole. I held a lighted torch in my right hand and wore a white palm-tree chaplet with its leaves sticking out all round like rays of light.
>
> The curtains were pulled aside and I was suddenly exposed to the gaze of the crowd, as when a statue is unveiled, dressed like the sun.†

*See J. Trachtenberg, *Jewish Magic and Superstition* (New York, Meridian Books, 1961).

†Lucius Apuleius, *The Golden Ass,* trans. by Robert Graves (London, Penguin Books, 1950), p. 286.

Figure 65

The figure shown on the World trump is probably that of the initiate being presented to the populace. He is dressed as Mithra himself. In Mithraic terminology, he was now considered *pater*, "father."

Through identification with his hell-harrowing deity, Mithra, Dionysus or even Persephone, the initiate had entered into communion with the divine parent, considered as either the great god or the great goddess, Zeus or Demeter. "I and my Father are one" claims the mystical Jesus, echoing the words of Dionysus. "I am the true Vine"—the words of the divine Bacchus. "I am the Bread of Life"—so was holy Persephone, the Corn Maiden. Both Dionysus and Jesus had conquered death. So had their initiate, in and through them.

Figure 66

The transformed initiate or reborn shaman had thus reached a mystical identification with the moving spirit of the universe, that *anima mundi* of the Neoplatonists. He had become one with Aion, the vital spirit of the universe according to the Gnostics, that quintessence of the alchemists. He was master of the four elements. According to Marcus Messala, a Roman consul writing around 53 B.C., Aion, the transformed Mithra, was in fact Janus, even as reborn Dionysus was Zeus and Persephone Demeter.

A later feminine counterpart to all-encompassing Aion was Isis, who, according to Neoplatonists like Robert Fludd, represented nature herself. In an illustration to his work *Utriusque Cosmi Historia* (Oppenheim, 1617), she is portrayed as standing as an intermediary between the universe and the absolute, with one hand pointing aloft whence a chain joins her to the Tetragrammaton; the other hand is chained to the rotating spheres of the cosmos beneath her feet, passing on the divine influence. She is God's executrix. (See Figure 65.) This is a possible explanation of the twin rods of the Waite trump, though not a very likely one.

Similar designs occur on Templar coffers originally from Burgundy but preserved in the private museum of the Duc de Blacas and described by the writer Baron Joseph von Hammer-Purgstall.* Androgynous figures wearing mantles and the crenellated crown of Cybele or Hades, sometimes flanked by Sun, Moon and stars, hold up twin chains through which the influence of these heavenly bodies descends to earth (see Figure 66). Sometimes beneath the figures' feet lie skulls flanked by five-, six- or seven-pointed stars. The weird beings are undoubtedly further versions of the Aion, in this instance portrayed hermaphroditically, containing the powers of both mother and father within them.

Whether the triumphant initiate who has returned from death be identified with the god or goddess, Aion or Isis, Zeus or Demeter, the mystical end result was thought to be the same. As with the yogi who guided his awareness up and then down the pillar of magical chakrams in his spine and the Siberian shaman who clambered physically up his birch tree to heaven and returned with messages from the Sun and Moon, so the true magus, the mystery initiate, brought tidings from worlds of the gods to the world of men. In him were vested the very powers of nature herself. He had conquered the underworld and heard the music of the spheres. He now returned to tell of it.

Hardly surprisingly, the traditional interpretation of the World trump is "prize" or "reward." The Fool has become the master; the pawn, king. The saint has received his crown.

Whether the prize be a longed-for goal, the powers of the magus-mind, or simply monetary recompense, the World is, all in all, the best card in the deck.

Reversed it implies a sense of permanence rather than bounty, some say stagnation. But I feel this is a false interpretation. For the World is the Aion, whence derives our word "eon." It is thus a symbol of cosmic time, the completed pattern and final perfection of man and enterprise alike.

And what better note to end on?

*See Thomas Wright, "The Worship of the Generative Powers During the Middle Ages of Western Europe," in *Sexual Symbolism* (New York, Bell Publishing Co. and Julian Press, 1957), pp. 133-44.

Appendix:
A Note on the Minor Arcana

Though the suit cards appear to play very little role in the story told by the trumps, they do appear to show a tantalizing similarity to those "four magical treasures" of Celtic lore: the spear of Lug, the caldron of the Dagda, the sword of Nuada and the stone of Fal. W. B. Yeats, A. E. Waite and Jessie Weston all noted this similarity, and Waite even went so far as to hint darkly that the key to this tarot mystery lay hidden " . . . in certain secret records now existing in Europe. . . . "* Whether his secrecy was bound up with an initiation oath of some sort or merely due to his own magian sense of mystery-mongering is difficult to tell.

If the four tarot suit signs do connect in some way these legendary treasures, then additional insights immediately present themselves besides the more obvious feudal interpretation of cup-priest, sword-warrior, coin-merchant and rod-worker. For instance, the spear of Lug may well have been the prototype for the miraculous spear of Longinus as it appears in the legend of the Holy Grail.

In turn, the spear appears to have been a modification of an even earlier Celtic symbol, the club of the Dagda (a giant father-god) the wielding of whose phallic rod brought death or healing depending on which end was used. It would correspond with the tarot Rod in our scheme.

The death-dealing sword of Nuada, on the other hand, shows the male potency in its destructive aspect. Zeus' thunderbolt, Saturn's sickle and the Green Knight's ax all appear to be similar symbols, comparable to the tarot Sword.

The tarot Cup would obviously refer to the Grail and its Celtic forerunners, the caldrons of the Dagda and Ceridwen, deriving from Irish and Welsh lore respectively. In all instances they are symbols of divine inspiration and fertility.

*See A. E. Waite, *The Holy Grail* (New York, University Books, 1961), p. 572, and A. E. Waite, *Shadows of Life and Thought* (London, Selwyn and Blount, 1938).

The Coin, our last remaining tarot emblem, pairs off with the stone of Fal, the holy coronation seat of ancient Irish kings. The stone of Saint Columba, a cross-incised stone common to old Celtic churchyards and Anglo-Saxon leech-books, is closely associated with it. It has been suggested that the Stone of Scone, which rests beneath Saint Edward's Chair in Westminster Abbey, is in fact the original stone of Fal.

The Siege Perilous, that chair in which only the true High Prince could safely seat himself, was the Christianized version of the stone in Arthurian legend. Like Saint Columba's stone, it too was discovered floating on the water in a miraculous manner.

Whether the Minor Arcana emblems do in fact have anything to do with the four treasures is very difficult to prove. The shared symbolism is the theory's strongest point. As in all sorcery, the final answer may turn out to be a pragmatic one: if the theory works, then use it!

Bibliography

Some of these works are mentioned in the text, others not. Unfortunately many of them are extremely rare and available only in certain museums. Taken together they form an excellent background to the subject for those wishing to pursue the tarot mysteries further. Of those works readily available, the books of Gertrude Moakley and C. P. Hargrave are to be particularly recommended.

Though not dealing specifically with tarot cards, the books of D. P. Walker, Frances Yates and E. M. Butler are extremely valuable explorations of medieval and Renaissance magical beliefs and their pagan ramifications.

Tarot Cards and Mnemonic Systems

Brockhaus, H. "Ein Gedulspiel, die Leitung der Welt oder die Himmels-leiter, die Sogenannten Taroks Mantegnas vom Jahre 1459-60," in *Miscellanea di storia dell'arte in onore di I. B. Supino*. Florence, 1933.

Court de Gébelin, Antoine, *Le Monde Primitif analysé et comparé avec le monde moderne*. Paris, 1781.

Gerard Encausse, "Papus," *Le Tarot des Bohémiens*. Paris, 1889.

Hargrave, C. P., *A History of Playing Cards*. N.Y., Dover, 1966.

Lévi, Eliphas, *Le Grand Arcane, ou l'occultisme dévoilé*. Paris, 1898.

Luria, A. R., *The Mind of a Mnemonist*, trans. by Lynn Solotaroff. N.Y., Discus Books, 1969.

Marcolini, Francesco, *Le Ingeniose Sorte*. Venice, 1550.

Mathers, S. L. M., *The Tarot*. N.Y., Occult Research Press, no date.

Moakley, Gertrude, *The Tarot Cards Painted by Bembo*. N.Y., New York Public Library, 1966.

Ovid Moralisé, Konegelige Bibliothek, Copenhagen, m.s. Thott 399.

Peter of Ravenna, *Phoenix, sive artificiosa Memoria*. Venice, 1491.

Regardie, Israel, *The Golden Dawn*, 4 vols. Chicago, Aries Press, 1938.

Ridewall, John (Johannes Ridovalensis), "Fulgentius Metaforalis," in *Studien der Bibliothek Warburg, IV*. Leipzig, Berlin, 1926.

Sermones de Ludo cum Aliis. Fifteenth-century illuminated manuscript in the collection of the United States Playing Card Co., Cincinnati, Ohio. No author or date.

Seznec, Jean, *The Survival of the Pagan Gods*, trans. by Barbara Sessions. N.Y., Harper Torchbook, 1961.

Waite, A. E., *The Pictorial Key to the Tarot*. N.Y., University Books, 1959.

Weston, Jessie, *From Ritual to Romance*.

Yates, Frances, *The Art of Memory*. London, Routledge and Kegan Paul, 1966.

———*Giordano Bruno and the Hermetic Tradition*. London, Kegan Paul, 1964.

Yeats, W. B., "Red Hanrahan," in *Early Poems and Stories*. N.Y., Mac-millian, 1925.

Mythology and Folklore

Apollonius of Rhodes, *The Voyage of the Argo*, trans. by E. V. Rieu. London, Penguin Books, 1959.

Apuleius, Lucius, *The Golden Ass*, trans. by Robert Graves. London, Penguin Books, 1950.

Aristophanes, *The Frogs*, trans. by B. B. Rogers. Loeb Classical Library, 1924.

Bible, King James Version.

Budge, Wallis, *Egyptian Magic*. N.Y., University Books, no date given.

Cartari, Vincenzo, *Le Imagini colla sposizione degli dei degli antichi*. Venice, Marcolini, 1556.

Cellini, Benvenuto, *Autobiography*, trans. by George Bull. London, Folio Society, 1966.

Cicero, *De inventione*, trans. by H. M. Hubbell. Loeb Classical Library.

Cumont, *Recherches sur le Manicheisme*. Brussels, 1908.

Euripides, *The Bacchae*, trans. by A. S. Way. Loeb Classical Library, 1912.

Filelfo, *Canzone Moralé*. Florence, 1431.

Frazer, Sir James, *The Golden Bough*. London, Macmillan, 1922.

Graves, Robert, *The Greek Myths*. London, Penguin Books, 1955.

—————*The White Goddess*. London, Faber & Faber, 1961.

Illuminated manuscripts referred to in text for iconographic reference:

ms. Douce 134, f.83, Bodleian Library, Oxford, England.

ms. fr. 143, *Livre des echecs amoureux*. Bibliothèque Nationale, Paris.

ms. fr. 6986, Bibliothèque Nationale, Paris.

ms. Urb. Lat. 1398, Vatican Museum, Rome.

ms. fifteenth-century *Miniature of the Holy Grail*. Bibliothèque Nationale, Paris.

Ovid, *Metamorphoses*. London, Penguin Books.

Plato, *The Symposium*, trans. by Jowett, 2d ed. Oxford, 1890.

Sophocles, *Oedipus at Colonus*, trans. by Robert Fitzgerald in *Sophocles, the Oedipus Cycle: An English Version*. Harvest Book.

Vermaseren, M. J., *Mithras, the Secret God*, trans. by T and V. Megan. London, Chatto and Windus, 1963.

Sorcery and the Cabala

Abano, Pietro d', "Heptameron Oder Elemente der Magie," in J. Scheible, *Das Kloster*, Vol. 3. Stuttgart and Leipzig, 1846.

Agrippa von Nettesheim, Heinrich Cornelius, *De Occulta Philosophia*. Antwerp, 1531.

Albertus Magnus, *De Mirabilibus Mundi.* Cologne, 1485.

Barham, R. H., *The Ingoldsby Legends.* London, William Clowes and Sons, 1880.

Barrett, Francis, *The Magus.* New York, University Books, 1967.

Butler, E. M., *Ritual Magic.* Cambridge University Press, 1949.

Casaubon, Meric, *A True and Faithful Relation of What Passed for Many Years Between Dr. John Dee and Some Spirits.* London, 1659.

Estienne, Henri, *Discours Merveilleux de la Vie, Actions et Departements de Catherine de Medici.* 1575.

Fludd, Robert, *Ultriusque Cosmi Historia.* Oppenheim, 1616.

Ginsburg, C. D., *The Kabbalah.* London, Longmans, Green & Co., 1863.

The Greater Key of Solomon trans. by M. Mathers. Chicago, DeLaurence, 1914.

Griffith, F. L., and Thompson, Herbert, eds., *The Demotic Magical Papryus of London and Leiden.* London, 1904.

Ibn-Khaldun, *The Muqaddimah,* trans. by F. Rosenthal. London, Routledge and Kegan Paul, 1967.

Lévi, Eliphas, *Transcendental Magic,* trans. by A. E. Waite. London, Rider, 1896.

The Picatrix, trans. into German by H. Ritter and M. Plessmer, in *Studies of the Warburg Institute,* Vol. 27. London, University of London, 1962.

Regardie, Israel, *My Rosicrucian Adventure.* Chicago, Aries Press, 1936.

Scholem, G. G., *Major Trends in Jewish Mysticism.* New York, Schocken Books, 1961.

Trachtenberg, J., *Jewish Magic and Superstition.* New York, Behrman's Jewish Book House, Inc., 1939.

Trithemius, Joannes, *Steganographia, hoc est, ars per occultam scripturam animi sui voluntatem absentibus aperiendi certa . . . Darmstadii,* 1606.

Waite, A. E., *Shadows of Life and Thought.* London, Selwyn and Blount, 1938.

Walker, D. P., *Spiritual and Demonic Magic.* London, Warburg Institute, University of London, 1958.

Witchcraft and Shamanism

Burland, Cottie, *North American Indian Mythology.* Feltham, Middlesex, England, Hamlyn House, 1965.

Castaneda, Carlos, *The Teachings of Don Juan.* University of California Press, 1968.

Curtis, Natalie, *The Indians' Book*. New York, Harper and Bros., 1923.

Deren, Maya, *Divine Horsemen: The Voodoo Gods of Haiti*. New York, Chelsea House. 1970.

Eliade, Mircea, *Shamanism, Archaic Techniques of Ectasy*. New York, Bollingen Foundation, 1964.

James, E. O., *The Ancient Gods*. London, Weidenfeld and Nicolson, 1960.

Maple, Eric, *The Dark World of Witches*. London, Robert Hale Ltd., 1962.

Proceedings Against Alice Kyteler. London, Camden Society Publications, 1843.

Robbins, R. H., *Encyclopedia of Witchcraft and Demonology*. London, Spring Books, 1959.

Scot, Reginald, *The Discouverie of Witchcraft*. London, 1665.

Seabrook, William, *Witchcraft*. New York, Harcourt, Brace, 1940.

Wright, Thomas, "The Worship of the Generative Powers," in *Sexual Symbolism*. New York, Bell Publishing Co., 1957.

Parapsychology and Related Fields

Dean, E. D., "Plethysmograph Recordings as E.S.P. Responses." *International Journal of Neuropsychiatry*, Vol. 2 October, 1966.

Eastlake, Charles, *Goethe's Theory of Colours*. London, John Murray, 1840.

Fox, Oliver, "The Pineal Doorway" and "Beyond the Pineal Doorway." *Occult Review* (1920).

Galton, Francis, *Inquiries into Human Faculty*. London Macmillan, 1883.

Jung, C. G., *The Interpretation of Nature and the Psyche*. London, Routledge and Kegan Paul, 1955.

_____, *Psychology and Alchemy*, trans. by R. F. Hull. London, Routledge and Kegan Paul, 1963.

Muldoon, Sylvan, and Carrington, Hereward, *The Projection of the Astral Body*. London, Rider, 1951.

Osis, Karlis, and Turner, Malcolm E., Jr., "Distance and ESP: A Transcontinental Experiment." *Proceedings of the American Society of Psychical Research*, Vol. 27 (September, 1968).

Rhine, J. B., *The Reach of the Mind*. London, Faber & Faber, 1948.

Sudre, René, *Treatise on Parapsychology*. London, George Allen and Unwin, 1960.

Vernon, J. A., *Inside the Black Room*. New York, Clarkson N. Potter, Inc., 1963.